Reversing the Deal Flow

The Secret to Prospects Calling You
to Become Clients

SARANO and BROOKE KELLEY

AUTHORS
Sarano Kelley and Brooke Kelley
The Kelley Group International
founder@kelleygroupintl.com
www.thekelleygroup.net
Tel: 866.584.8885

PUBLISHER
High 5 Communications, LLC
info@high5communications.com
Tel: 435.750.0062

ISBN: 978-1-945578-12-0

TABLE OF CONTENTS

Dedicated to Martin Shafiroff

The Secret to Reversing the Deal Flow

Imagine your assistant getting frequent calls from prospects asking to meet with you to become clients. You wish you could meet them and review their finances, but first you need to decide if they're a fit for your practice and whether you can find time in your schedule.

The prospects tell your assistant they can accommodate your schedule, but say they'd like to see you sooner rather than later. Unfortunately, sooner doesn't work because you're so booked out with business opportunities that, even though these prospects have substantial assets, they'll have to wait.

This is what business development looks like for an advisor who has "reversed the deal flow." When you build a well-organized network of advocates for your practice, they'll spread the news about you and send referrals your way. You'll then reach the point where prospects are calling you asking to become clients. This is what reversing the deal flow means.

To achieve this you'll need to follow the detailed steps in this book in their exact order. The strategies in this book are like rungs on a ladder, and by putting one foot in front of the other, you can ascend to unimaginable heights.

The process will propel you to celebrity like status. Think about the ridiculously long lines outside of Apple stores when a new product is released, or a hit musical like "Hamilton" where people are clamoring for tickets that cost an arm and leg (if you can even find one). This is not a bubble phenomenon like the Tulip Bulb Market Bubble of the Netherlands in the 17th century or the tech bubble that burst in 2000. It is a process built to endure. Reversing the deal flow happens when your brand reaches the highest marketing success possible and is sought after by many. Some advisors become so well known for being the best at what they do that they define a marketplace — or even create one.

Is your phone ringing off the hook right now with new, qualified prospects wanting you to manage their money? Does it sound like a fantasy? I must warn you that unscrupulous advisors like Bernie Madoff were able to use this process for devious means. We can't do anything about that, but we can do something about helping ethical, hard-working advisors like you become champions of this process and ensure that the "good guys" win. While ethical behavior and investment performance don't determine the deal flow, how much and the way you market does.

In the past decade, my business partner and wife, Brooke Kelley, and I have been doing just that for some of the most successful financial advisors in the U.S. and Canada. Our purpose is to see to it that the best advisors become the best-know advisors in the industry so they can make a difference, not only in the lives of clients and the people they touch, but in society as a whole. This is our passion, and success is our track record.

Don't Keep Your Practice a Secret

Many financial advisory practices are run by ethical, intelligent and extremely competent advisors who are serving their clients well and doing all the right things … except for one. They are keeping their practice a well-kept secret, and that is not a compliment. The reality is, these advisors sometimes fall prey to the illusion that because they are so ethical, because they're so well intentioned, and because their clients love them, they don't need to promote their practice. This way of thinking is understandable, but they will soon realize they are not attracting the high-quality referrals they need to grow their business.

Even the best and biggest brands make it a point to promote their businesses through every channel imaginable.

People can't select you as an advisor if they don't know you, and the degree to which people know you is not an opinion — it's a statistic, and numbers don't lie. Right now, there are likely hundreds of people who actually know you and know what you do and what you offer, and those are the only individuals who can select you as an option. Of those individuals, only a certain number currently need your services and are a fit for your business. While this may be obvious, it is the obvious that is most easily overlooked and hidden from view.

Remember, nothing stays in a steady state. Your business is either growing or contracting. That means if you are not actively promoting your business, your brand is shrinking whether you realize it or not. It's like gaining weight — you don't see it creeping up on you until you step on a scale.

Keep Prospecting

When you first became an advisor and started prospecting, you probably experienced an incredible growth rate — 1,000, 2,000, 3,000, and even 5,000 percent. However, you were already up 100 percent just by opening one account. When you opened up two accounts you were up 200 percent. But eventually this growth rate begins to cool, and then stagnate, seemingly under invisible pressures.

Over time, you have become busier handling a larger list of clients and prospecting often becomes a "want." Even though you may want to grow, unfortunately "wants" do not require a response. They aren't like "needs" that trigger an immediate response because they can lead to an emergency — like when you first started in the business and were concerned about not bringing in enough client assets to be able to support you and your family. You remember the good old days, don't you, when the simple math was "no prospect, no eat"? The reason top advisors reach such astronomical success is because they have an ongoing focus on the growth of their business.

Before I was in the business, I read Robert Shook's *Ten Greatest*

Salespersons that includes a chapter about a man I consider one of the greatest advisors of our time, **Martin Shafiroff**[1]. I met Marty early on in my career. After entering an Ivy League college at age 16, I landed at 44 Wall Street as a cold caller. I paid my cold-calling dues and became a stockbroker at Lehman Brothers in the office of this great advisor. In my first year, in the early 1980s, I did $400,000 in production. That same year Marty was said to have done $20 million in production. He has reportedly since done as much as $80 million in production in a single year.

Several years ago, some of our coaching students went to New York to visit this $80 million producer. They told us that while they were waiting to speak to him, he was clearly on the phone prospecting. Even after 40 years in the business and undoubtedly $100s of millions in production, he was still prospecting — billionaires!

In one of my keynotes I sometimes say: "Do you want to know what 40 years of prospecting would be worth in our business? The answer is $80 million in production in a single year." Brooke and I have coached quite a few of Barron's top advisors, advisors from top firms and many advisors from the private wealth side of the business. It never ceases to amaze us that 99% of the coaching requests we receive come from the largest producers. Wouldn't you think they'd be the last advisors who feel the need to prospect?

If you're new in the business, our career advice for you is: Don't stop prospecting. Wipe from your mind the idea that prospecting is just a short-term price to pay. It's fundamental. In the sports world, it's like blocking and tackling or putting and driving. Think of it like brushing your teeth. You wouldn't go without brushing your teeth, would you? You wouldn't say to me, "Coach, I was just too busy to brush my teeth," or "You know, something came up and I didn't get around to brushing my teeth." Consider this: There are people in the

---

1 Shafiroff, Martin has nearly $10 billion AUM and is featured in the book *Ten Greatest Salespersons* authored by Robert Shook, published by Harper & Row Publishers, Inc., 1978.

advisory business for whom prospecting is like brushing their teeth — and they are monsters in production.

The Art and Science of Being Connected

In the financial advice business, the most sought-after advisors tend to be the ones who are socially well connected. You might think that you have to be born into a high-status family or environment to be well connected, but in reality, it's a condition that can be created. If you look around, you'll notice that there are two specific professions in which people constantly work on the craft of being connected. One is a politician and the other is a socialite (or celebrity). These are individuals who study the science of being connected and have turned the science into an actual art. This same art can be applied to an advisory practice.

Again, this is not a role you're born into. Instead it's something you design to become connected with the right people and to reverse the deal flow. So instead of merely chasing prospects, they will be knocking on your door because they've heard about you or someone in your network has referred them. How do you learn how to do this? We teach a form of marketing that we refer to as "conversational or dialogue marketing." It's a script you use to add new connections to your social network of clients, family, friends, COIs, strategic partners and more. We'll provide powerful examples of this type of dialogue in the pages of this book. If you're a casual reader, you will get immense value out of reading this. If you're serious about growing your advisory practice, then welcome back to the training camp … this is your playbook!

Brand, Message, Audience

Developing a well-known brand is not solely a matter of high ethics or investment performance; it's a marketing discipline. We know many advisors are frustrated with popular financial-media gurus who probably couldn't fight their way out of wet paper bag let alone advise the public on investing. Despite their poor advice, their opinions are well promoted — much to advisors' dismay.

Brooke and I see it as our mission to make sure the best, most ethical and most client-focused advisors are armed and able to excel beyond their competition.

Exhibit A shows a triangle diagram that illustrates the relationship between three areas critical to the success of this marketing process:

Exhibit A

At the peak of the pyramid is the word Brand. On the right is the word Message, and on the left is the word Audience.

You may think you have a unique brand, but it doesn't matter how exceptional that brand is if it cannot be articulated as a unique message. That unique message is only going to be valuable to your unique audience, which is made up of the people who are most inclined to do business with you. This is a key concept because many advisors are either off-message or off-audience in their marketing. They might spend a lot of money and energy on their efforts, but if they don't have a clear message or aren't targeting the right prospects, their results will be dismal.

You may have to shift your thinking to adjust to this process. In all likelihood you've spent thousands of hours studying investments, watching the stock market, getting certifications and designations, poring through prospectuses, and going to due diligence meetings and product presentations. A typical advisor spends thousands of hours studying investments and has probably read hundreds of articles and books on the subject.

How many books have you read from cover to cover on marketing — specifically, marketing as it relates to an advisory practice? Most advisors would have a hard time counting them beyond one hand. I think we'd all agree that it's difficult to be an expert on a subject that one has not studied. In this business if someone's really good at managing investments but not good at promoting their practice, how well will they do typically? The answer is: Not well. They will fail.

Let's begin with some basic questions. First: Have you ever fallen prey to the idea that if you just do a great job, you don't need to ask for referrals or promote your business because people will simply spread the good word about you by word of mouth?

We've found that in many cases this rational, yet erroneous, notion has become a cover for not dealing with your discomfort in prospecting, which is really a lack of study, training, practicing and coaching. But we'll get into that later.

Here's a second question: How many people currently see it as their responsibility to promote your brand? How many people wake up in the morning, wipe the sleep out of their eyes, chug back a cup of coffee and think, "Wow, I can't wait to promote my advisor's brand?"

The answer: Only a few. When we've posed this question to advisors we coach, their answer is generally four to 10 people at most. Those people usually include the advisor, members of their team, perhaps a few proactive clients and one or two centers of influence who consistently refer business to them.

This group represents an asset to your business because they are brand ambassadors, and they also represent an off-balance-sheet asset. You can look at it as having your own sales force, and what they're promoting is you. You are the product. Wouldn't you like more of these types of people promoting you and your services?

Reversing the Deal Flow

The likely low number of people promoting your brand means there's work to be done. To reverse the deal flow, you have to confront a very simple statistical fact — the number of people who see it as being beneficial to them to actively promote your brand will have to increase dramatically. How much? Somewhere between a factor of 10 to a factor of 100. (In our experience, this is a safe bet.) Let's say you have 20 people promoting your brand; your goal might be to increase that to 200. There is no doubt in our minds that advisors who have used our process over the last decade now have hundreds of people promoting their brand. We want you to have that goal. Keep in mind, marketing, even more so than selling, is about "the law of large numbers." Direct mail, advertising, and even cold calling take huge, repeated efforts to produce a return.

Now for the "how." The way to increase your brand ambassadors or advocates is to have a well-organized social network. You currently have a core social network promoting you and your services, but you must better organize and grow this group. You need to present a clear and portable message about your practice that these ambassadors can easily convey to others.

The formula for success is not just to exponentially expand the number of people actively promoting your brand, but to do so in a precise order. In my keynote address, you will hear me say repeatedly, "If you do the right thing but in the wrong order, it will still be the wrong thing." You'll want to assign your advocates specific roles and functions that will give you the widest and deepest reach possible into the populations of people you most want to work with. In this book we use the art of conversation to build and expand your audience through the medium of a well-organized social network.

Targeting a specific niche enhances your ability to broaden your networking base. The more connected the individuals in that niche are to each other, the more they influence each other. The more they communicate with each other, the quicker you will statistically be able to reverse the deal flow. But ultimately it will be up to you to put your unique spin on these marketing strategies and dialogues — the "secret sauce" that will create an inflow of referrals to your practice.

The Evolution of an Advisor

This book will explain the marketing evolution of a financial advisor and his or her practice. In it you'll learn 11 of the 34 steps and dozens of dialogues for making the process work. (Additional steps are included in Vol. II and III.) You'll be starting at the lowest level of marketing, which is Producer, and progressing to Rainmaker. In Vol. II you'll progress to Dealmaker and in Vol. III on to Connector, and finally to Renowned Expert. An advisor must climb each step on the marketing ladder, in sequence, to reach the highly prized top status.

As a **Producer,** you must master certain fundamental strategies such as cold calling, approaching a stranger, and social networking before moving up to the next level. (See Assessment Grid on page xxi.) If you don't have a good understanding of or don't attain the skills featured in any of these steps, your practice won't grow systematically, and you'll fall short of reaching your goals. *Someone who has a very mature practice and very solid skills at the lower level of the ladder can begin at a slightly higher starting point in this process.*

Rainmakers have an existing book of clients, but they are still actively engaged in growing the practice. Rainmakers must be able to grow their business in the most efficient way possible, because they're also managing the business. Conversational-marketing methods like asking for referrals from clients and centers of influence are really the providence of the Rainmaker.

Advisors who rise above Rainmaker status are considered **Dealmakers**. While producers and Rainmakers generally acquire relationships one at a time, Dealmakers are not interested in "onesies" or "twosies" — they are interested in being recipients of large blocks of assets flowing in from multiple sources. It's no surprise Dealmakers are forever thinking about forming strategic partnerships with people from both inside and outside their firm. At the end of the day, they're looking to make a deal.

Connectors move up the ladder and widen their marketing reach by working with networking groups, joining clubs, getting involved in associations, and sitting on charitable boards, as well as other similar strategies. They become connected through these various groups to the prospects in their chosen market niche. These connections bring in referrals.

At the pinnacle of the marketing ladder are advisors who are **Renowned Experts.** These advisors have the widest range and the longest reach. If you view them in a game of strategy, such as chess, these Renowned Experts are the chess pieces that can make the widest moves and cover the greatest distance — the most versatile pieces on the board.

At this zenith, advisors will find themselves receiving a steady inflow of high-quality referrals from a variety of targeted sources. Like politicians or socialites, they will have learned the art and science of magnetism, and prospects will be naturally attracted to them and their practice. They have mastered the process of reversing the deal flow.

Get Ready!

After decades of careful development, testing, and working with more than 250,000 advisors, we wrote this guidebook to help our coaching clients, trainees and you! However, be aware that the bar of excellence has been raised. It is not enough to understand the theory behind this process, to know the underlying pattern, learn the dialogue order, use the right words or hone your listening skills. While all these things are important, your level of conviction, honesty, and authenticity will be tested. How heartfelt your communication is, your use of eye contact, voice, handshake, how well you remember names and other critical details, how you handle difficult people, reclusive people, evasive people, distraction, noise, your ability to appropriately get out of conversations that are not in alignment with your goals and ethics… all these things need to be confronted.

In other words the warm up is over; you are being given the playbook. You're expected to show up fully suited and ready to play. Get ready, it's going to be gritty. However, by implementing each of the steps you're taught in this book, eventually you will attain the same title I ascribe to Marty Shafiroff[2] — The Master. It is an honor to be your coach.

❖❖❖

---

2 Shafiroff, Martin has nearly $10 billion AUM and is featured in the book, *Ten Greatest Salespersons* authored by Robert Shook, published by Harper & Row Publishers, Inc., 1978.

Volume 1:
Achieving the Status of Rainmaker

E levating yourself from a Producer to a Renowned Expert requires completing a step-by-step process in which you master a list of 34 comprehensive marketing/communication strategies laid out in this three-volume series.

Exhibit B

In Vol. I, you will be rising from Producer to Rainmaker by completing the first 11 steps of the total assessment. In Vol. II, you will follow steps 12 to 18 to elevate yourself from Rainmaker to Dealmaker. And in Vol. III, you'll move up the rungs to Connector and finally to Renowned Expert, completing steps 19-34.

The strategies, or steps, must be completed in sequence before you qualify for a higher status level. The levels are shown in Exhibit B. But before you jump into the steps, you must first assess how well you are currently executing on these marketing/communication strategies. We use this same exercise with every advisor that interviews for a spot in our 18-month coaching program using the Reversing the Deal Flow system. This way they know where they were before the program started, and they can see where they are after completing the program.

What you're assessing is:

• To what degree you are currently marketing your practice

- How proficient and successful you currently are with the marketing/referral methods you're using
- How many marketing/referral methods you're using

At the end of the process, you will rate yourself again. Undoubtedly you'll find the amount of marketing you do, the number of advocates you have in your networking system promoting your brand, and the number of methods you are using will increase exponentially.

To begin, read through the following descriptions of the steps to understand how to rate yourself on the 11 strategies contained in Vol. 1. Next, rate yourself on a scale of 1-10 using the grid on page xxi to determine the degree to which you are marketing yourself and your financial services practice.

Producer: The Starting Level

(Complete steps 1-11 in the assessment grid using the definitions below to see where you are as a Producer.)

1. **Cold Calling** – To what extent are you leveraging calls to prospects either through a "mass" calling campaign or with more targeted calls to people who don't know you?

2. **Walking Up to a Stranger** – How successful are you at starting conversations with strangers in a wide range of contexts and turning those interactions into business development opportunities?

3. **LinkedIn Outreach** – Are you calling people who want to "link in" with you or those you want to reach out to on LinkedIn and successfully establishing cross-referral relationships or closing business?

4. **Social Networking (face-to-face)** – How well are you taking advantage of social networking groups to connect with your ideal prospects or your prospects' centers of influence?

5. **Friends, Family and Social Acquaintances** – How successful are you at approaching people close to you and asking

them to become your clients or to refer prospects?

6. **More Business** – To what degree are you managing all of the assets of each of your clients?

7. **Different Business Solutions** – To what degree are you leveraging your firm's full range of investment solutions and offering them to clients?

8. **Bigger Business** – How comfortable do you feel asking your existing clients for the largest amount of business possible? How successful are you at getting the biggest business you can from current clients?

9. **Recovering Lost Clients** – To what degree have you been able to recover a lost relationship, and do you know what to say to get them back as clients?

10. **Removing Non-Optimal Clients** – How successful have you been in transitioning your non-optimal relationships to another channel or advisor while keeping them as fans of you and your practice?

11. **Repricing Conversations** – To what degree are you able to get clients onboard with a new repricing policy? How effectively and aggressively is your business priced? Do you avoid discounting everything you can just to get a client?

Becoming a Rainmaker

The maximum score possible on the first 11 steps of the assessment scale is 110 (a score of 10 for each strategy). The purpose of this evaluation is to identify the strengths and weaknesses in your current marketing strategies so you know where improvement is needed. You can then dig into the steps in this book to learn ways to strengthen and expand upon the marketing and referrals strategies that you've deemed as weak.

Don't feel discouraged by what you haven't been doing. The key is that you now have a step-by-step process to follow instead of a scattered list of random marketing ideas you might like to try … someday. This process will not only lead to referrals flowing into your practice, but increase your passion for what you do and the satisfaction you feel when working with your ideal clients and select partners.

These activities will put you in touch with many inspiring people along the way: clients, COIs, colleagues, connectors, and others who will have a personal and professional impact on your life. Brooke and I have been amazed at the incredible advisors we've met during our careers and the way they have profoundly touched our lives. Consider this book your ticket to the greatest practice building ride you've ever experienced. Hold on to your seats… let's start!

◆◆◆

Exhibit C

MARKETING/ COMMUNICATION SKILL	1	2	3	4	5	6	7	8	9	10
	Least <----------------------------------- Use of Strategy -----------------------------------> Most									
1. Cold calling										
2. Conversing with strangers										
3. LinkedIn outreach										
4. Social networking (face-to-face)										
5. Friends, family and social acquaintances										
6. Getting more business										
7. Different business solutions										
8. Bigger business										
9. Recovering lost clients										
10. Removing non-optimal clients										
11. Repricing conversations										
12. Referrals from clients										
13. Client survey referrals										
14. Centers of Influence (COIs)										
15. Intimate events										
16. Client advisory board										
17. Mastermind group										
18. Business development group										
19. Board of advisors										
20. Mentor										
21. Strategic alliances										
22. Strategic partners										
23. Networking group										
24. Clubs										
25. Associations										
26. Charities										
27. Connectors										
28. Journalism										
29. Publishing										
30. Public Relations (PR)										
31. Speaking/Seminars										
32. Podcasts										
33. Radio										
34. Television										

WELCOME PRODUCER

You're on your way to becoming a RAINMAKER!

By completing the 11 Steps listed below, you'll start the process of Reversing the Deal Flow. Prospects will be lining up, asking you to take them on as clients.

STEP 1. Cold Calling

STEP 2. Walking up to a Stranger

STEP 3. LinkedIn

STEP 4. Social Networking

STEP 5. Friends, Family and Social Acquaintances

STEP 6. More

STEP 7. Different

STEP 8. Bigger

STEP 9. Recovery

STEP 10. Removal

STEP 11. Repricing

CHAPTER 1

Organizing Your Marketing and Referral Strategies

Marketing is a broad and varied topic that includes the many ways financial advisors can promote themselves and their practices. Certainly, advertising is part of the equation. Firms may promote their advisors through advertising, and individual advisors may send out direct mail. But from our perspective, the most important part of marketing is social or conversational marketing that involves voice-to-voice and in many cases, face-to-face communication between the advisor and a prospect. That could mean something as basic as cold calling or something as advanced as designing an elaborate strategic partnership.

Conversational marketing is about dialogues, and in this book we are going to largely examine dialogues and the strategic order in which they should take place. While many firms have libraries of resource materials on marketing, provide informational websites and offer instructions on the marketing power of social media, what is lacking is a well-ordered approach to conversational marketing. To better understand our definition of "well ordered," you might view each marketing approach as a "pearl." However, as Brooke says, without a well-ordered process there is no necklace. This is where we come in.

But before we get into more detail about marketing methods and the ordering of your marketing strategy, it's important to define the structure we use to guide advisors toward successfully implementing the various strategies. See Exhibit 1.1 below.

Exhibit 1.1

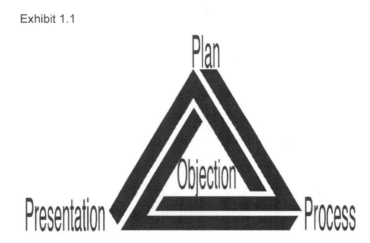

PLAN — For each strategy discussed in the book, you will need to come up with a detailed "plan." And that plan should include who you're going to talk to and details such as when you're going to meet with them and how the meeting will be arranged.

PROCESS — A plan won't matter if you don't have a "process" to put it into action. The right process will ensure your plans don't lie around gathering dust. It took us 25 years to perfect the process known as The Game,[1] which is used to coach advisors across the industry. It is a clear example of "process" because an advisor can turn any plan into a game or process and execute it with precision. The core driver of The Game is accountability, and your process will need to contain some sort of an accountability factor if you're expecting to be successful in your execution.

PRESENTATION — The third point of the triangle is "presentation," which is a script to be used to carry out the plan and process. While we often hear distain for scripts and scripting, realize that "making things up as you go" is not only unprofessional, it can be counter-productive because it wastes a prospect's time and turns them off. Sure, some advisors are successful in speaking off the top of their heads, but it can lead to inconsistent messages and may leave out important details. I often ask advisors at presentations on this subject to raise their hands if they like movies, and everyone raises their hands. When they put them down, I say: "So you love scripts — you just hate bad acting!" They inevitably get my point. Of course, using a script doesn't exonerate you from being well prepared before opening your mouth and inserting the proverbial foot!

Well-respected and high-profile businesses provide a consistent product. And in this case, I'm not referring to the investments offered, I am referring to you, the advisor. You are the product. Hence, you need to standardize communication the same way that you standardize all of the important processes of your business. The great thing about being able to deliver something of high quality in a consistent fashion is that you can then customize it to fit the individual and at the same time be absolutely sure that what you have customized will work.

Have you noticed that in many political campaigns, no matter what question a candidate is asked, the response always harkens back to their core message? Such is the practice of great communication.

---

1 *The Game: Win Your Life in 90 Days*; 2014; Kelley, Sarano; The Kelley Group Intl.

While some people may dislike this approach, what they often don't realize is that it's designed to make the message memorable. A good example of this is MacDonald's restaurant. Their process is well timed and honed, including how employees communicate with customers. What if you went into a McDonald's restaurant and the person behind the counter interrupted your ordering to tell you about their relationship troubles. That would be weird, and I'm sure you wouldn't appreciate the interruption, nor would the other customers.

While you may not think of yourself as a mass producer of things, keep in mind that you, like most people, hate an inconsistent product; therefore, the more consistently you can deliver, the better the customer experience.

OBJECTION — In the middle of the diagram is the word "objection," which you should think of as predictable, reasonable concerns and issues that people have and that you should be prepared to address. It is unfortunate that advisors are trained (if trained at all) to think like "salespeople" as opposed to concentrating on what salespeople really are — which is "great communicators." I like to use the term salespeople because it reminds us of our "roots" and our purpose, which is to ensure that valuable goods and services are provided through the process of communicating or selling. Objections should not be viewed as obstacles. Instead, they are simply the issues and concerns that are preventing individuals from getting what they need and should have, and which you are well qualified to provide. This is not a small difference in point of view.

A Well-Designed Marketing Strategy

The other key to marketing an advisory practice is the need for order. In other words, advisors who lack an orderly strategy will try a little bit of this and a little bit of that, doing none of it well or completely. The secret that very few advisors know is that a well-executed strategy is only effective because it is done in the right order. There is an innate order to the way an advisory practice expands its reach and marketing process, leading to the penultimate marketing achievement … to reverse the deal flow.

This is what Brooke means when she tells advisors they "have a lot of great pearls," but they "don't have a necklace." Often consultants, coaches or asset managers come to overly busy advisors with the marketing idea "du Jour" or the latest tip or "best practice." These solutions are presented as a "silver bullet" and come with a story about a top producer who "knocked the cover off the ball" with this latest and greatest idea. While the advice is well intentioned and advisors are grateful for any solution they can get, they're often poorly informed.

With the pressure of a competitive marketplace on your back, it can be hard to stick to a well-organized and disciplined approach that requires effort, repetition, measurement, adjustment and constant application. In sports or business, the formula for success is often the same: It's about discipline and a maniacal, methodical almost incomprehensible level of constant application that will result in your competition waking up one day and wondering how you just came out of seemingly nowhere and blew them out of the water … which was our plan all along.

In one of our many keynote presentations on Reversing the Deal Flow, we ask advisors: "What are two examples of marketing strategies that require no change in schedule, investment of money or additional time?" How would you respond?

One of the correct answers advisors most often give is "referrals." However, the second one — which they almost never guess right — is what we call socializing. We're not referring to social media or social networking (both of which require the scheduling of additional time). What we mean is the way most advisors engage in a wide range of social activities. For example: They're involved in their kids' schools; they participate in civic, religious, political and other groups; they belong to clubs; they are constantly around people.

All marketing strategies take a certain (average) length of time to "close business." If you compare "asking for a referral" to "walking up to a stranger and starting a conversation," which do you think takes longer? Clearly, "walking up to a stranger" is a longer close because that person doesn't know or trust you.

This highlights the fact that some strategies take longer and some take a shorter amount of time, and hence what emerges is an order — a hierarchy. What determines the order in which you should engage in marketing strategies? The right order starts with the strategy that takes the least amount of time and money, has the shortest sales cycle and is the most profitable. Other strategies will follow on a gradient-scale basis.

Organizing Your Marketing Strategies

The right order of a well-thought-out strategy is measured in dollars, the statistic of money. If a strategy is going to take a long time to bring in money, then that is not where you should focus your immediate energy. Instead you should "build up" to that strategy.

Look at the strategies listed below and put them in order starting with the ones that would take the least amount of time, effort and money to those that would take the most:

- Intimate Events
- Centers of Influence (COIs)
- Referrals from Clients
- Friends and Family/Social Acquaintances

If you ordered them correctly, you would see the items above are in the reverse order of what they should be.

Friends and Family/Social Acquaintances is first because these people know you and trust you, hence it shortens the sales cycle.

Referrals is the No. 2 strategy in this sequence — even over COIs. Most people think the top strategy should be "referrals." However, while the person referring someone to you may know and trust you and is evidence of your (the advisor's) success because you manage their money, the person they're referring to you doesn't. This means while the prospect will be favorably disposed toward you because you have a credible third-party endorsement, they will still need to get to know you and come to trust you.

COI's are next in the sequence. They can be very credible, but because you likely don't manage their money, there is a reality gap. This gap is so palpable that despite a COI's recommendation, a prospect may wonder "what's in it for the COI?" When the person referring you is a client, that way of thinking is rare. That's why COIs are the third strategy

Brooke's Notes

Whenever I ask advisors how they're marketing their practice you would be surprised how often someone who's looking for us to coach them says their wife (or husband) is upset because they spend so much time on Boards and other such activities for business development purposes making it hard to balance their lives. When I ask them how much in assets they bring in from Boards and how often, they seem to get a little defensive, and when I ask them how long they've been working to monetize the strategy, that's when they start to wonder if they might be making a mistake.

The lower strategies don't just fund the higher strategies, they pave the way, build the necessary audience and create a base. This is why the process resembles politics ... you are building a base.

in this abbreviated sequence.

Intimate Events falls last. Why? The biggest issue with any event is getting the right people in the room, and in this strategy sequence, your friends, family/social acquaintances, client referrals and COI referrals would all be the people helping to bring the right prospects to your intimate event.

These are "pearls of wisdom" — and together they make a necklace. The correct order would be:

1. Friends Family/Social Acquaintances
2. Referrals
3. COIs
4. Intimate Events

What we're sharing here is not rocket science, but you don't know what you don't know. Most people recognize that a publisher is not going to publish a book if the author doesn't already have an audience, the same way no sponsor is going to put money behind someone who doesn't have a following. In the world of marketing, as in the world of politics, it is the solidity of your base that allows you to expand your reach.

Mind Dumping

To avoid these frustrations and failures, we recommend advisors start with an activity known as "mind dumping." (We also use this method in our 90-day coaching program based on our bestselling book, *The Game*.)

The process is easy, and simply involves putting everything in your head down in an Excel spreadsheet. In mind dumping, the last thing we want you to think about or worry about is order. In fact, quite the opposite, we want you to explode with marketing ideas. We want you to write down every tip, best practice — even bad ideas — in the "A" column of an Excel spreadsheet.

The key is not to do any editing. There is to be no decision making. There is to be no judging. Typically, you cannot do this in a single sitting, so give it some time. When I do this exercise, a day later I might see a billboard or I'll be at the airport and see a commercial out of the corner of my eye, and some incredible breakthrough idea will come to me that I add to my notes. The list can evolve over days, weeks, and even months.

For example, you might write down, "I need to update my LinkedIn profile. I need to join a local business group that I found through social networking. In the spring, I would really love to do an outdoor event for my clients." Later, out of nowhere, a strategy will emerge that uniquely combines these disparate thoughts into an elegant strategy.

Where might other ideas pop into your head? You may be at a conference and hear another advisor talk about their marketing success stories. You might be reading a magazine unrelated to financial services and come across a brilliant insight about marketing. Where do you put this information? And when you need it, how will you get to it? Mind dumping is a simple solution. The bonus is, it helps your mental function by freeing you of all the creative thoughts and ideas you've been trying so hard to retain in your brain — taking up valuable space.

Once you feel like you have a substantial list, go to the B column on your Excel spreadsheet and rate on a scale of 1-10 how much **time** you believe each idea will take to accomplish. The easiest way to do this is to look through the list, find the item that you think would take the most time and mark it as a 10. Then find the item you think would take the least amount of time and mark it as 1. Then use that as a gradient scale to rank everything inbetween.

Next go to the C column and think about the **cost** of each activity. Assign a 1 to the item that has the lowest or no cost and a 10 to the most expensive idea. Finally, in the D column, rank on a scale of 1-10 the degree of effort needed to accomplish these activities, again with 1 being the least effort and 10 being the most.

Now when you go back to your spreadsheet, you have a list of ideas and activities ranked in a way that makes it easy to decide what to try first. This makes your list much more approachable and much more doable.

Now, you'll move to the next column to further label the activities. Which of these items will be "**recurring**" and which are "**projects**?" Typically in the E column you will put a "P" next to something that looks like a project, which means it has a finite amount of steps to complete. Mark items with an "R" for recurring if they require more ongoing activity. For example, updating your LinkedIn profile is a project. Writing a newsletter is recurring. Having an annual golf outing for your client is recurring. Having a retirement party for one of your clients, unless you do this repeatedly, is a project. (See Exhibit 1.2)

Exhibit 1.2

ACTIVITY	TIME	COST	EFFORT	R/P
Update LinkedIn Profile	1	1	1	P
Golf Outing	10	9	7	P
Newsletter	7	5	8	R

Now take a look at the projects that take the least amount of money, time, and effort and see which of those you can most quickly accomplish. Also, determine if any projects or activities can be delegated to an assistant. Now you've started to reduce the amount of traffic and noise in your head and have a list of ideas to draw from that you can execute on a gradient scale.

Developing a Campaign

Ideally, at some point you will have moved from the most profitable and easily produced projects on your list to recurring activities. Here is where you have the opportunity to put together a special marketing project that typically is also recurring. This particular activity is one of the critical ways to help you reverse the deal flow. It's what we call "campaigning." As you build your client base and employ marketing approaches that express your interests, passions and purpose in life, you will find that campaigning is one of the most important strategies you can use to build your brand.

So there are some projects, like having an annual golf outing, that are considered recurring. Now think beyond the purpose of the golf outing as a client appreciation and prospecting event and tie it to raising money for Alzheimer's awareness, because many of your clients are concerned about this issue. You might also hold the golf event during National Alzheimer's month. That's what we call a "campaign." Campaigns tend to have themes. They often are a way to build audiences, and they can have a level of power beyond what we see in some other marketing approaches.

Many people who include campaigns in their marketing plans understand that ultimately the way to reverse the deal flow is not so much through selling, or simple marketing, but through campaigning. Fundamentally, selling is always going to be a contact sport and a numbers game and will depend on your willingness to engage in both of those activities. Marketing usually involves a certain level of strategy combined with a high level of activity, along with the law of large numbers. Campaigning requires a lot more horsepower, but it can propel a business way beyond what any short-term activities can expect to accomplish. A campaign speaks to the heart, soul and mind of a particular audience. Of course, the right campaign is going to be the one that really means something to you — that really does matter to you.

If you take on the mentality that you are running for office and these prospects are your constituents, the biggest blunder you can make is to be unknown. Whether these prospects work with you now or later, the goal is that one day they will work with you. Certainly they should hear about you and know about you. This of course, is a very high level of brand awareness and marketing success.

Why is it that the largest producers have a maniacal focus on prospecting? We'll discuss what I learned from my own mentor, who reportedly did as much as $80 million in production annually. I know your question is, "What in the world could someone do for 40 years that would be worth $80 million a year?" The answer is: prospecting business development every day for 40 years straight. Most of us would have to admit that our own prospecting has periods of peak activity and then periods where our efforts were something quite less than that.

If you boil it down to basics, the income you earn is a direct reflection of the production you do. The production you do is a direct reflection of the assets that you manage, or in some cases, the products that you sell. We submit that the assets an advisor has under management is a direct reflection of the amount of business they are proposing. In our coaching, we ask advisors to report every week to us publicly how much in assets they brought in during the prior week as well as how much business they proposed and how many referrals they received.

How many advisors (besides those we coach) do you think typically know how much in business they are proposing? The answer is, in most cases, very few. You might think, "Well, isn't it enough that I know week over week how much in assets I'm bringing in?" The answer is, "Absolutely not!" Here's the problem: The assets that you bring in are a lagging indicator. They only tell you about the past. They don't tell if you're on track or doing the right things now.

Let me put it this way, if $50 million came in, would that be a good day or a bad day? Most advisors would say that's a good day, but the reality is, it's actually a bad day. How could it be a bad day? The answer is simple: If $50 million comes in today, that means your pipeline has now been reduced by $50 million. Let's say it took six months for you to get that $50 million into position. What happens when you receive that $50 million is you get so ecstatic about the success that in most cases you stop doing the strategies that brought that money in. Now it might take another six months before you realize you fell off the prospecting track, and then you lose another six months getting your pipeline flowing again.

The Importance of Tracking and Keeping Stats

The most astute and successful advisors aren't necessarily the ones who merely have great ideas and strategies, they are the ones who know how to execute and keep a keen eye on what works and what doesn't. The largest producers have a maniacal focus on prospecting and typically have an intuitive understanding of marketing statistics. They realize that earning referrals takes a methodical approach.

The value of statistics is critical for every aspect of your business. At The Kelley Group, we look at our clients as a business we're investing in, and we look for coaching clients who are willing to run their business like a business. The role we take on is Chief Virtual Marketing Officer to the practice, and we operate as though our work results will be reported to senior management, investors or the Board, all of whom are not interested in anecdotal stories or good intentions. They want to see the cold, hard facts, and they know "numbers don't lie."

When it comes to marketing, statistics are king. They are the single arbiters of truth. We make it mandatory that everyone we coach keeps track of certain statistics. This becomes especially important in the realm of marketing where you need to be able to test and refine your approach until you have discovered what works best for you.

Many advisors appreciate the coaching rule we've established, which is "first you master *our way* and then you're free to do it your way" whether

It's asking for referrals or using the best script for a cold-calling campaign. The point is, once you master our way, we want you to come up with a better way, understanding that our way is a floor not a ceiling.

As co-heads of marketing for your advisory practice, you and I are likely to have moments when you think your idea or way is better than mine. How will we hash out our differences of opinion? The answer is, the numbers will decide. The numbers will tell us the truth. Suppose we coach you to say things one way when you close an intimate event and set people up for the next step in your process. However, you disagree and have another script in mind. Well, conduct a study. We will ask you to do one event with your script and then another event with our script. The script that leads to the most meetings wins!

Let's say you have a question about a particular approach. Try using one approach on 10 people; try a different approach on 10 other people. Which one gave you the better return? At the end of the day, what's right is what works. But for you to truly know what works, you must be willing to conduct your own marketing study – just like any professional business owner would.

Never Lose Track

If you look back at the amount of assets you've received in a given week, it's like looking in a rearview mirror. If you want to know whether you're on a growth track and if you're doing the right things to increase business, then you need to look at how much business you are proposing week over week. In other words, when you increase the amount of business you propose, you will increase the amount of assets you receive because you now have a conversion ratio. Unfortunately, most advisors don't know how much business they're proposing on a weekly basis, and they typically don't know their closing ratio. That means their business planning is largely based on guessing.

Here's another way to look at it. You raise your hand at a shareholder meeting to ask the CFO this question: "Excuse me, sir. I'm a shareholder in your company, and I represent a lot of investors. My question is, what's the current size of your prospecting pipeline, and historically, how much of that will convert in a single quarter into earnings?" The CFO looks at you rather shocked and says, "Well, I don't know, but you have to understand we're working really hard, and after all, we're very, very busy." Would you invest your money in a company like that? Of course not. Would you run your business like that? I hope not.

In most cases, statistics will tell you if a business is going to go up or go down. How do they do this? The answer is a simple variable: Number of sales (or referral) calls. Typically, the more sales calls a person goes on, the more business they propose. More specifically, the more you increase the number of sales calls you go on, the more you increase the number of people you get in front of, and the more you tend to increase the amount of business you propose. You increase assets, production and income.

So how many sales calls a week do you think most advisors are going on now compared to what they were going on when they first started? The answer is, too few. As we go around the nation speaking in front of large groups of producers, people are honest enough to admit that in many cases they may go on only two or three sales calls a week. Contrast that to when they first started and were going on two to three sales calls a day. Yes, there are challenges in managing your day-to-day practice, but don't lose sight of the activities that revved up your practice in the first place.

In the beginning, you probably relentlessly tracked the number of contacts you made, the numbers of meetings you had, the number of people who attended your seminars, and the number of follow-ups you made. However, when you reached a level of some comfort and success, did you stop tracking your own activity and instead started tracking the market or something you couldn't control? If so, that's when you made a critical mistake. Your success is not determined by market statistics, it comes from metrics related to your individual business, and those are the statistics you must know in order to reverse the deal flow.

Conclusion

Once you build a robust pipeline, you're in a position to build a successful practice. Look at the number of sales calls you go on every day or every week and the amount of marketing and prospecting you're engaged in, and that will determine how many warm opportunities you have. The number of opportunities determines how many sales calls you can set, and the number of sales calls determines how much in new business you can propose.

The important principle you need to remember is to tackle the right marketing method in the right order. The advisors we coach learn our marketing mantra: "If you do the right thing but in the wrong order, you are still doing the wrong thing." When advisors choose to engage in marketing in an arbitrary manner, it not only causes failure, but frustration.

Never lose track of how you built your business in the first place.

◆◆◆

CHAPTER 2

Reframes

The Art of Overcoming Resistance and Handling Objections

The ability to change a person's mind is a unique and powerful skill. It is its own discipline that transcends science and becomes an "art." We address this important topic because we find that, statistically, many marketing and referral strategies involve handling an objection. You will hear us emphasize again and again that objections are issues, concerns, and considerations that a client or prospect needs to have addressed by an advisor. Objections can block a sale and prohibit you from reaching your personal goals. We will provide you with a powerful set of tactical communication skills to handle all types of barriers that hinder the sales and marketing process.

During two decades of coaching some of the most successful financial advisors and studying the largest producers in our industry,

Brooke's Notes

The skill set of overcoming resistance and handling objections comes from a complete system of communications skills we teach on how to powerfully and systematically conduct a sales call using face-to-face consultative selling and presentations skills. While they are not a part of this book, the two are very necessary and reflect the old adage that "sales is a numbers game and a contact sport." The two most important aspects of one's sales performance are 1) increasing the number of people you're in front of by increasing the amount of marketing that you do to get in front of prospects, and 2) having a well-thought-through, documented process for how you're conducting your sales calls.

we have found that one of the key factors for their impressive success is their ability to communicate effectively. In fact, people are often surprised to learn that the top one percent of advisors often don't have advanced designations. Instead, they have excellent communication skills and are great at relationship building and handling people. One of the most advanced skills exhibited by these advisors is the ability to handle resistance and objections as if they were a puzzle to be solved, or in some cases, a fun game. You can achieve this ability to handle objections through practice. To master it, you will need to practice it to the point of flawless delivery.

Sales: A Numbers Game and A Contact Sport

All of our coaching clients are required to track and report to us certain statistics on a weekly basis. Two of the most telling statistics are: 1) the number of qualified sales calls made week by week and 2) their closing ratio. These two numbers tell us immediately if the advisor is getting "up to bat" enough and if they're making contact with the ball. If you're not getting up to bat enough and your contact with the ball is poor, then you must fix those two things before you do a rain dance or hire a sales voodoo doctor to see if a curse has been placed upon you.

It is common knowledge that people enjoy doing what they are good at and vice versa. For example, if you enjoy cooking it's probably because you're good at it. In truth, most advisors do not enjoy handling objections and resistance. Why? Because they don't like dealing with the strong issues prospects have with their recommendations, and they are ill prepared to address them. In other words, they're not good at it!

It may seem a bit strange to say that advisors don't enjoy handling objections because they are ill prepared, especially when they encounter the same (relatively limited) objections day after day. In most cases, when faced with resistance either on the part of the client or prospect, an advisor's gut reaction is to push back (or resist) — a process we call "invalidation."

Here's an example. Most salespeople in a retail environment will walk up to a customer and use the well-worn opening, "May I help you?" Customers have learned a predictable answer to this question that typically sends the salesperson away: "No, I am just looking." Although it is often an automatic response, a good salesperson will honor it and find another way to engage the person in conversation or make an effort to understand what they really meant. Later in this chapter we will discuss how to do this.

That being said, it's hard to imagine that an intelligent person could regularly encounter the same objection or resistance and continue to handle it in a way that is bound to create an unsuccessful outcome. Yet that is often the case in retail settings. Why? The answer requires a deeper understanding of sales and human behavior. When a person encounters a challenging situation, inevitably the person is looking for a way to survive and succeed in that situation.

Consider the example of an advisor calling a referral or prospect who says, "I'm already working with someone, and I'm very happy with him." Often when faced with this situation, advisors fall back on the response: "I'm sure you'll agree that it makes sense to get a second opinion," — not the best response.

Keep in mind that people with an objection are the best type of prospects because when you do change their minds, they will fully understand what you are proposing or selling and know that you have appropriately addressed their issues.

Handling Objections: A Valuable Sales Tool

Handling objections is an integral strategy used in marketing. This is why my keynote presentation on "Handling Objections" has been rated No. 1 at conferences for the three largest advisory firms on Wall Street.

Handling objections is an important skill from a statistical point of view, and this book is ultimately based on and is all about statistics. In sales, after thoughtful "discovery," you will have to offer a solution or recommendation. Whenever you make a recommendation, there are only four possible responses:

- Yes
- Question
- Maybe (an objection)
- No

Here you start to understand the science of selling, which is really the science of communication. On a percentage basis, you'll find that you get very few "yes" or "no" responses. (Although many people think they get more "no" answers than they actually do.) When it comes to questions and objections, the latter are the most challenging to handle successfully.

The list of responses on page 22 forms a hierarchy because the goal is to get a "yes." From there, the scale descends to lower probabilities of a successful sales outcome. While "yes" is great, it can be extremely satisfying to answer an important question someone asks and then hear a "yes" response. We all enjoy helping others, and that's why we've invested so much time in our given expertise.

Notice that a "maybe" response is the same as an objection because all objections are a maybe. An objection means that the person is undecided. This is an excellent indication of interest and means that the person needs some clarification so they can get to either a "yes" or a "no." Getting a "maybe" or an objection is a net positive, not a negative.

Often salespeople become so rejection phobic, they hear "maybe" as "no." In my keynote presentation, I use the following example:

I ask an audience member, "What would you say if I asked you right now if you would mind if I hauled off and kicked you in the shins?" (I make it a point to stand close enough and start to wind up my foot.) I then ask them, "Would you say to me: 'Let me check with my wife, or would you say no?" In fact, most people say, "Heck, no!"

The point is, you know when something is a "no." I tell the audience that you could even choose to argue with me and say: "Coach, this person is 99% against working with me and only 1% uncertain." Then I ask, "So is 99% a definite 'no'?" The audience always gives me the same answer: "No!"

In the same keynote, I also propose a hypothetical situation that involves "heavy resistance." The scenario is one in which an advisor warm calls a referral, explains who he is and why he's calling. The referral responds: "I like you, but I have several advisors, and I even have a brother in the business. On top of that, I pay very little in fees. I think you're wasting your time."

Would you call that an objection or a "no"? If they don't say "N – O," then it's a maybe; it's not a straight "no." I often have the audience show me how they would handle this objection by videotaping the person sitting next to them while he or she recites it to them, and then they record their response to the objection. (You might try this.)

It's often humbling for them to see themselves rambling, talking on and on, being defensive, biting their lip, and lacking real enthusiasm or gestures as they respond. No one does this intentionally, and most of the advisors I coach have never watched themselves handle an objection or observed the two biggest mistakes a person can make when handling an objection. The first is, most advisors have an objection to the prospect having an objection. We say: Put yourself in the prospect's shoes. The "objection to the prospect having an objection" comes across as blatant disrespect. Imagine if you were trying to sort something out and the person who was supposed to help you was covertly hostile or, even worse, belittling you because you had the nerve to voice concerns and didn't just roll over and say "yes."

The second big mistake advisors make is not listening as the prospect shares his or her concerns. Instead they are already focused on giving them their "spiffy" canned response. No wonder prospects feel like the advisor couldn't care less about them and what they're trying to sort out.

We all can appreciate what it feels like to be on the receiving end of such treatment, but it's hard to see that on a bad day, in an off moment, or when you're simply not at your best. Any of us can make these mistakes. Brooke will definitely confirm that on a bad day my communication skills leave a bit to be desired.

In the Reversing the Deal Flow process, there are two sensitive communications that must be mastered: 1) the handling of objections and 2) the right way to treat people when we need to decline working with them. These are the two areas where ill will can be created and can undermine your desire to become a well-known and well-regarded resource to a specific client niche.

A Learned Sequence

When working with clients, it is even more important to turn them around or get them to understand a particular recommendation because you, the advisor, are often blamed if something goes wrong, or if something goes right and you couldn't convince the client to take your advice. Why do intelligent people keep using the same approach, which rarely ever works, hoping for a different outcome? This sounds a little like the definition of insanity, or maybe temporary insanity. You use your normal coping mechanisms for handling objections to deal with something you may not fully understand.

For example, if you encounter a difficult situation, you may form an immediate objection or resistance that comes across as defensiveness or a comeback. This is a habit pattern, and is how we mechanically operate when faced with a challenging situation or problem.

This book is designed to assist you in establishing a training pattern, or a learned sequence of steps designed to optimally impact a situation. In the case of handling objections and resistance, the training pattern is as follows:

Step 1: The Objection — The individual objects or resists: *"I have several advisors, plus my brother's in the business and because of that I pay very little in fees. I think you're wasting your time."*

Step 2: The Advisor Replay — You replay the objection: *"So you have family in the business, and you have several advisors. The last thing you are probably looking for is another advisor."*

Step 3: The Verification — The client or prospect verifies the accuracy of the replay or will correct it with: *"Yes that's what I said"* or *"No that is not what I meant. What I meant is ..."* (Notice that this is a training sequence and at various steps, such as this one, there are only a few options.)

Brooke's Notes

If you follow the strategies in this book, understanding that the goal is to get each strategy in place on a stable basis and then to grow the next strategy on top of the former strategy, you can't help but end up with a more robust pipeline. This is not our opinion; these are statistical facts.

Step 4: The Acknowledgment — You "acknowledge" the person for their objection or resistance: *"I am glad that you feel you can be open and honest with me, it's the only way to get the best outcome for you."* You could also say, *"I want to thank you for being up front"* or *"I want to acknowledge you for your candor."* Stay away from acknowledging people with phrases such as *"I understand"* or *"I appreciate"* because they can come across as patronizing or gratuitous.

Step 5: The Probe/Reframe — You then use a special class of probes designed to "reframe" the way the prospect or client is relating to their own concern or issue. Reframing is a communication process often used in therapy to help people who are unable to overcome a problem or difficulty. It is different from a rebuttal, which is a way of countering a person's argument. Unfortunately, most "popular" sales training programs view the prospect as an adversary to be overcome or a sales dialogue as an argument to be won. Rather, it's a process of helping people clarify their needs, their thinking on how to fulfill those needs, and providing the expertise needed to understand the options and arrive at a good decision.

There are reframes used to handle two types

of objections: the conscious and the subconscious. A conscious objection is one in which an individual seems to have a rational or logical issue with what is being proposed and may not yet see the "whole picture." The subconscious objection comes from someone who has an emotional or illogical reaction to a given scenario.

These objections can be addressed using the "lead in" phrases below. You can use these examples and others that will be provided in this book to come up with your own wording when handling a particular issue related to a specific strategy.

Conscious and Logical Reframes

The conscious reframes below are used when you believe you have the ability to "reason" with a person.

1. Appealing to Their Logic through Specificity: *"Can you be more specific/Can you give me an example?"*

2. Change of Referential Index: *"If you were me, how would you ...?"*

3. Comparative Past Violation: *"Has there even been a time in the past where you ... and it wasn't...?"*

4. Black and White Contrasting: *"What do you like the most about X (whatever the subject of the objection is)? Nothing is perfect, what do you think could be improved?"*

5. Appealing to a Higher Value: *"What's important to you about that? If there was another or even better way to achieve that would you be open to that?"*

6. Uncovering: *"What am I missing. I'm confused, help me out ..."*

7. Time: *"In (X period of time) how important will this seem"* or *"If we look out (X number of years) will you wish you had thought differently about this now?"*

Unconscious and Emotional Reframes

These reframes are used when the person you're talking to is obviously being emotional, irrational and illogical.

1. Extremes. Echo back the extreme phrase they have used so it sounds like a question, such as: *"Always?"* or *"Never?"* or *"Everyone?"* or *"No one?"*

2. Emotional Response. *"That really hurts,"* *"It makes me sad to hear you say that,"* or *"I am deeply disappointed in myself that you could feel that way."* If the emotion is in the background but unstated/suppressed: *"I sense concern,"* *"I sense something is wrong,"* or *"I sense some dissatisfaction."*

3. Humor. E.g., *"Can you take a joke?"* or *"That reminds me of something very funny I once heard..."*

4. Stories. *"This reminds me of a time..."* or *"That reminds me of a story..."*

5. The Take Away. *"I am not accepting 'no' as an answer, given that what are we going to do about this..."*

6. The Hail Mary. *"You definitely have a very good point, let's accept that and move forward."*

The key is not to feel as if any one reframe has to be the be-all and end-all. What you are dealing with is a very simple and powerful phenomenon, seemingly only understood by children and some of the most talented salespeople in the industry, and that is: Most people only have the ability to say no twice before they are forced to really think about what they are saying.

Saying "no" or "I'll think about it" is so automatic with people that often they are not truly thinking about what they are saying. If you go back to the phenomenon that a person automatically says no twice, why not give them at least a third chance to respond? The goal of this process is not for you to change their mind but to give them the necessary opportunity to change their own mind. You give them the chance to really think through what you are suggesting. Unfortunately, great advice is often not taken because salespeople are not persistent enough in their communication. On further examination, you'll find that many salespeople simply don't know how to communicate at a certain point without being rude or disrespectful, which is why they don't persist. They don't know what to say!

Handling a Non-response Using Emails and Voicemails

Emails and voicemails are an efficient way to communicate with prospects and clients, but if you don't get a response back, what should you do? Should you take it personally? No, but most of us do. How often has someone stopped communicating with you, and you assumed it was because of something you did or didn't do, only to find out later that it had nothing to do with you? I suspect this is often the case.

The first thing you should logically assume when someone doesn't return your email or voicemail is that the person didn't receive the message. Here are a series of email messages to send out when you don't hear back from a client or prospect:

Step 1. The subject line of the first email should read:

"Missed communication."

In the body of the email, you would write:

"Below is the email that I sent you. I just wanted to know whether or not you received this communication."

If you decide to leave a voicemail message, you would say:

"I was wondering if you got my communication."

Step 2. If you still don't receive a reply, the next step is to send another email with the subject line: *"Are you OK?"*

In the body of the email, you would write:

"I haven't heard from you and I'm concerned. I'm wondering if you are OK."

You want to make it clear that your concern is for the *person*, not the investment proposal or recommendation you were suggesting. Think about it this way: What's more important, the relationship or the transaction? Which one's more valuable? The answer, of course, is *the relationship.*

Step 3. If you still don't hear back from the person, your subsequent email subject line will read: "Is something wrong?" In the body of the email, you would write:

"Since you didn't respond to my prior email, I assume everything is OK. I'm wondering: Is something wrong?"

Step 4. If you still hear nothing from the person, the next email you send will have the subject line:

"Did I do something wrong?"

Your responses follow a gradient scale. You don't start off assuming you did something wrong, but as time goes on and your emails are ignored, you then have to consider that as a possibility. Remember, your ultimate goal is to re-establish communication with that person. There is no point in asking them about an investment you suggested if they're not even communicating with you.

We have coached advisors who have followed this response sequence and the results have been impressive. About 80 percent of the time, the advisors get apologies back from the client or prospect for not responding sooner. They then explain why they didn't respond, e.g., a family member was ill, they were on vacation, they had an out-of-town emergency, etc. Once they finally do respond to your email, you can re-open the lines of communication and renew the relationship — an even stronger one.

Conclusion

There are many approaches and countless great examples of reframes and their unique ability to change a person's perspective, and the lists we provided on pages 27-28 are in no way exhaustive. In this book, we are discussing the most frequent objections for each marketing strategy and the most effective reframes for addressing concerns.

It is not enough to know the strategies, the order they should go in and how to communicate them powerfully. It is equally important to realize that people will have concerns and issues, and you need to be prepared to handle them powerfully and professionally.

If you learn these skills, what difference will it make in your results and your enjoyment in handling the objections and resistance of clients or prospects? Was there ever a time you wished you had known what to say and didn't — so you missed a major opportunity? I'm asking these questions and pushing you because I know you want to be a better advisor.

If you were us, how would you go about building a better relationship with you? That reminds me of a story ...

◆◆◆

Reversing the Deal Flow

CHAPTER 3

STEP 1

Advanced Telephone Skills
Cold Calling

E ven though "cold calling" is not a widespread practice today, advisors can learn a lot in the way of verbal communication skills from examining and honing this sales approach. Just so we don't sound old school, we've decided to give this strategy a more modernized and relevant name: "advanced telephone skills." Yes, phone skills incorporate the fundamentals of cold calling, and rightly so. Cold calling tests your mental and verbal reflexes in ways that no other marketing strategy can. Even if you're never in a position to make a cold call, the question is: Do you understand the cues and motivations that make you incredibly successful when conversing over the phone?

Using a strategy like cold calling can be an uphill battle. Most prospects don't know you or the value of your services. However, as you progress through each step in this book, you are gradually gaining leverage, which means you are speaking to more and people who will take your call because they know you, either personally or by reputation.

Let me give you some background on myself that will help you understand why I believe it's critical to master the basics of cold calling — the foundation for advanced telephone skills.

When I was 23, I was a stockbroker at one of the top investment banking firms in the industry. Those were my cold calling days. It was the early 1980s, before cell phones and do-not-call registries existed. But I didn't have the benefit of social media searches, either. Every day I got 150 or so leads and was expected to make 500 dials or more a day and get five to 10 qualified leads. If I did not call the leads I was given, they were taken away. Translation: cold call or starve. I must admit, it was a motivating system.

I had to have five to 10 leads a day because I was expected

Brooke's Notes

As you near the end of the Reversing the Deal Flow process, people will be glad to hear from you and will be calling you before you call them. In fact, you'll need to train your assistant to be an effective gatekeeper, because prospects will be calling you asking to become clients, and not all of them will be a fit. Screening and qualifying prospects will become even more important as the demands on your time grow. This is where an excellent command of verbal communication skills can take you.

to open a minimum of 10 and, preferably, as many as 20 new accounts each month with qualified investors. That meant I was trying to make five to seven new account presentations a day to meet the minimum expectation.

One day the lead I received was "Steven Spielberg." Yes, I mean *that* Spielberg — one of Hollywood's greatest producers and directors. No matter whose name and phone number showed up on a white card, I had to call him — or else one of the other 40 competitive advisors pounding away on the phones would. There was nothing more embarrassing than someone else taking your leads.

I soon realized Steven Spielberg had eight gatekeepers screening his calls, and each one was tougher than the last. Finally, after a lot of blocking and tackling and matching their ever-increasing skill levels, I arrived at the eighth and ultimate assistant. I thought I'd run head long into an oncoming freight train. I couldn't get around or through her. I stuck with my script and increased my intensity, but she returned each volley by smashing the ball back into my face.

When I look back on it, it was a glorious battle, and I marvel at her quick mind and her expert communication skills. I will never forget her because she made me want to be better.

Fast forward to a decade ago when I was developing the Reversing the Deal Flow process. I decided to test the system on my favorite crash dummy: myself. I came up with a list of the seven people I would most want to meet and work with. I couldn't help but put Spielberg on my list. Even though I was wiser, older and polished, I prayed that Spielberg's eighth assistant had taken early retirement so we wouldn't have another "Thrilla in Manila."

Then one day I signed on with a major national foundation to support an effort I'm passionate about, global poverty. I had cold called my way into the foundation's strategic partner department and told the head of the unit that I thought I could do a better job promoting their multi-billion dollar fundraising efforts than they could. They took a meeting with me, probably figuring I was either extremely passionate… or crazy.

I told them I had devised a process for reaching anyone, so they gave me a list of billionaires and their blessing to recruit them for donations, and of course, Spielberg was one of them. All I had was a list of names — not even a phone number — but it was all I needed. I did my due diligence work and put the strategies in this book into practice. I gained the support of many people, including some billionaires, but Spielberg still eluded me.

I was working with a friend and mentor who was the CEO of another well-established nonprofit. (Mentoring is one of the strategies detailed in Vol. II.) I happened to bring up my frustrations about not being able to reach Spielberg. While I try not to bring up my petty problems with the great people who have helped and guided me in my career, that day I was in a bad mood and I slipped.

He asked me how I was feeling and I let my guard down by saying, "I suck." When he asked why, I responded with, "I've been trying to reach this guy for three decades and I'm still nowhere."

My mentor was a tough, well-trained lawyer and here I was wasting his time. I felt like I had overstepped my boundaries by talking about my Spielberg predicament.

At that point he asked to put me on hold. I was on hold for a very long time. Now I was both humiliated and covertly angry.

When he came back on the line he said: "Write down this date and address." I did as I was told, even though I was confused. He then told me that he had scheduled a meeting for me with Spielberg's right-hand man. The meeting was scheduled at the back lot of Universal Studios, and I was to meet him in the building with the original "Forrest Gump" bench outside.

I was stunned. I hung up the phone and told Brooke, "I think we just got the meeting we wanted with Spielberg." I wondered how that happened so easily. How could this person who had eluded me for so long be just one meeting away?

I share this story to illustrate that my early cold calling strategy was a "numbers game." I made up for my lack of leverage with a massive number of phone calls. Communicating with prospects changed from being difficult to being simple and rewarding. My life had changed in other ways, too. I started out with no social network, no connections, and no leverage. What I did have was purpose, intent and the willingness to develop a skill set, and that made all the difference.

Here are four tips I want to share with you about mastering phone skills.

1. Practice, Practice, Practice

In my early days, my colleagues and I were required to memorize a script and read and learn the Lehman Brothers rebuttal book. I made sure I was prepared before I got on the phone. I was trained, I was drilled, I was recorded and I was coached.

I anticipated every possible reaction or rejection to my script, and I tracked how much time each call took. I spent countless hours in the mirror practicing "rebuttals" (this was before I learned the art of "reframe" from my linguistics trainer who worked for the intelligence community).

Through this training and practice, I formed a rule known by our coaching clients as the "100 reps." The rule is that every technique or script is to be practiced 100 times in a mirror. You need to know your lines by heart so you can give your full attention to a prospect without worrying about how you sound or what you'll say next. You learn how to become a professional communicator.

2. How Do You 'Appear' Over the Phone?

I was schooled in the "theatre of the mind." What is that? Let me answer it this way. When we train advisors on advanced telephone skills, we ask, "What do you think you can tell about someone just from hearing their voice over the phone?" Your answer might be: a person's gender, attitude, intelligence, mood and whether they're paying attention to you.

But what about facial features or the color of their hair? Yes, this may sound ridiculous, but people actually do picture the way a caller looks as they talk to them. This is the reason why when you meet people you've only spoken to over the phone, they may not look the way you think they should. The point is, the way you express yourself over the phone forms the image of you that people see in their mind's eye and determines how credible they think you are. For a true professional, there are no casual calls. Every call you make is a performance, every word is carefully chosen, and every presentation is honed to create the best possible representation.

3. Physical Actions Affect Your Voice

The reason behind "smile and dial" (smiling when you talk on the phone) is that your facial expression actually creates the undertones in your voice. Someone who is "smiling" sounds like they enjoy what they're doing. There is also an unconscious assumption that people who sound happy are attractive, successful, honest and competent. If someone sounds unhappy, you would make the opposite assumptions. This is why we conduct a voice analysis with our coaching clients, bringing out the best in their communication skills.

4. Do You Have Command?

When you're on the phone, you want to come across with authority, which means you want to present a commanding image. This can seem antithetical to cold calling because many new advisors probably don't feel like they're in command of the conversation. However, we stress a different kind of command: command of yourself.

This means being in command of your attention to others. Are you paying attention to the person on the other end of the line and totally immersed in the experience? Or are you getting distracted by your surroundings? We tell our coaching students, "We want you to pay attention to your attention." If something or someone doesn't have your full attention, you are the victim of distraction.

When you're on the phone with a prospect: Are you standing and gesturing? Are you controlling your body and is it fully engaged in the moment, or are you engaged in distracted, fragmented body movements? You need to be in control of both your mind and body. If you are, then you have command.

As a quick note, when people (both men and women) are prospecting, their testosterone levels tend to rise because prospecting or business development requires a bit of aggression. You have to be on your toes, not back on your heels. If you are afraid, reluctant, complacent or mediocre, you lack an edge.

Campaigns

When you call on prospects, no matter what the outcome, you are becoming "known." Even if the prospect is not interested in working with you at that time, they will likely remember your name or something you said. We call this campaigning because you are planting seeds that can grow and provide a bountiful harvest in the future. The concept behind campaigning is: "Either you will work with me now, or you will work with me later, and you will know my name." Not being known is much worse that being rejected. What you say to your prospects must be memorable.

What does your presence say about your commitment to action? If you are lackadaisical when calling, you come across as someone who is just going through the motions. Your lack of engagement, energy, and motion will suggest to a prospect: "Now here's someone who's going to waste my time, and I need to blow them off."

Finding the Zone

One of my most successful and enjoyable days of cold calling happened when I was spiraling down and couldn't get myself to make even 100 dials a day. If I didn't get my call reluctance under control, I pictured myself handing out flyers in front of Trinity Church and staring down Wall Street like I did when I first started in the business.

I had a "dialer," an intern whose job it was to get prospects on the line and then hand the phone to me. Normally he sat at a desk in front of me with his back to me. But I turned him around so he faced me and we were eyeball to eyeball. We couldn't avoid each other.

The dialer had one phone and I manned two phones simultaneously. At 8:15 a.m., we were ready to "Release the Kraken!" as Zeus (actor Liam Neeson) said in *Clash of the Titans* when unleashing a giant, violent sea monster. Whenever I got someone on the phone, I stood up, I stopped hiding, I stopped caring who saw me, and I stopped caring who hung up on me. Instead I focused on call after call and the love of the grind. I focused on the person on the other end of the line and what I needed to do to reach, not just their ears, but their mind.

When I finally put both phones down at the end of the day, I had made 400 "dials" and my intern had made 600. Not only that, I spoke to 125 contacts and qualified some 23 leads that day, breaking my old record. In fact, the lead total that day was higher than what I'd done the entire previous month.

I had discovered the ecstasy of being in the zone: the love of the phone and connecting with people, and the love of rapid motion and intent. It occurred to me that fear and rejection have a speed or pace. Rejection slows your pace.

This is how I discovered the Optimum Motion Scale that we use in our coaching programs. We sometimes refer to it in the coaching program as "hustling to get the ball." Let me explain. Emotions have a structure. You can feel them in your body. For example: sadness and depression are often felt from the chest down, whereas anxiety is often felt from the chest up to the head. Emotions have a relationship to time: regret is an emotion of the past, whereas anxiety is an emotion concerned with the future.

Emotions also have a relationship to speed, and motion and emotion have a correlation. If we assigned a rate of speed to an emotion, assuming that 1 is no motion and 12 is the most rapid motion, they would be ranked as follows:

12. Chaotic	**Moving too Fast**
11. Anxious	
10. In the Zone	
9. Ecstatic	**Success Levels**
8. Excited	
7. Self-Confident	
6. Tentative	
5. Concerned	
4. Doubtful	**Try Harder**
3. Depressed	
2. Apathetic	
1. Hopeless	

At the bottom of the chart is the emotion people experience if they don't even try to win — hopeless. Level 2 (apathetic) is when a person wants something but won't make the effort to go after it. Think of the Aesop's Fable of the fox who can't jump high enough to get some delicious grapes and decides that because he can't reach them, they must be sour (hence the term "sour grapes").

Level 3 (depressed) is a person who is in motion but finds it hard to get much done, or if they do, it seems pointless. Numbers 4 through 6 are emotions that cold callers often exhibit. They come across as weak because their doubt, concern or tentativeness comes through.

With these "lower" emotions, people are often working against themselves because they are fixated on the past. The slower the motion, the more they are hanging onto the past and the more energy they have to put forth to overcome their own inner resistance. In cold calling, this is death. For everyday calling, it's not much better.

At Level 7 (self-confident), their attention is much more "in the present," but a liability occurs if they are too self-focused, and hence self absorbed, so, they can't have the maximum impact. At Level 8 (excited), they put more attention on what they're doing and less on themselves. When you are at Level 9 (ecstatic), it is hard to say no to you. Your enthusiasm is infectious!

At Level 10 (in the zone), the voice in your head that has been slowing you and judging your every move is gone. You are in the zone, and when you are in that space, you can't be denied. Your intuition is on target, and your connection with people is electric. You see it with athletes when their will to win is so strong that they seem to overcome all odds. (How else did Tom Brady pull off a huge victory for the Patriots, coming from 25 points behind to win the Super Bowl in 2017?)

At Level 11 (anxious), you are moving too fast and things begin to worry you; at Level 12 (chaotic) you are moving so fast that you're feeling internal and external chaos. If you stay at a 12 for too long, you will eventually crash and fall back to Level 1 because everything will seem hopeless.

We tell our coaching clients that their goal is to live in the 7-10 range. We help them learn to identify when they need to speed up their pace and when they need to back off because their mind is starting to spin out of control.

When it comes to cold calling, sauntering doesn't work. You must hustle to get that ball! When you're not in the zone, your prospects will sense your lack of commitment and urgency and will respond accordingly with procrastination and disinterest.

Now that you understand how to focus your attention, use your body and facial expression as well as the role emotions play in cold calling, let's look at a few "plays" that will help you master this strategy. In many cases, you'll have to get through a gatekeeper, or someone who's keeping you from reaching your key prospect. This person is often a receptionist or personal assistant.

DIALOGUE 1

Getting through the Gatekeeper

Here's the wrong way to approach the conversation:

Gatekeeper: *"Good afternoon Mr. Jones's office."*

YOU: *"Hello, is Mr. Jones there?"*

Gatekeeper: *"May I ask who's calling?"*

YOU: *"Bob Smith."*

Gatekeeper: *"No, he's away on vacation. May I help you?"*

YOU: *"When will he be back?"*

Gatekeeper: *"On Monday. May I ask what this is in reference to?"*

YOU: *"It's a financial matter."*

Gatekeeper: *"Do you know Mr. Jones? Is this a solicitation?"*

YOU: *"Well ... er ... It's more personal in nature ..."*

Gatekeeper: *"Well, I'll have to take a message."*

As you can see, this doesn't end well. The process wasn't much fun either. The primary problem is that the dialogue turned into an interrogation because:

1. You didn't make a point to end the dialogue politely the moment you realized the person you wanted to reach wasn't there. You had nothing to gain by continuing.

2. The dialogue flow was "they ask you a question, you answer." If you felt like you were being interrogated, it's because you were.

Another wrong way to handle the conversation is to answer the gatekeeper's question with another question. You will come across as evasive, and the gatekeeper will need to question you. For example:

Gatekeeper: *"What firm are you with?"*

YOU: *"Is he in?"*

The better approach is to follow the simple rule of "answer a question, ask a question." Here's how the dialogue should flow:

Gatekeeper: *"Good afternoon, Mr. Jones's office."*

YOU: *"Hello, is Mr. Jones there?"*

Gatekeeper: *"May I ask who's calling?"*

YOU: *"Yes, this is Bob Smith. Is he in?"*

When the person asks, *"What firm are you with,"* you answer and then end once again with a question like, *"Should I hold for a few moments?"* Another approach you can use is to give a well-thought-out response as to why you're calling and continue with a question like:

"I only have a few moments to speak. Can you let him know I'm on the line?"

Never make an enemy of the gatekeeper. However, if you can't get past them, you can try "campaigning" or winning them over through other means. For example, in the first *Wall Street* movie, the only reason Bud Fox got in to see Gordon Gekko was because he had forged a phone relationship with the secretary and bought Gekko his favorite cigars for his birthday and hand delivered them.

Once you get through the gatekeeper and are on the line with your prospect, let's go over what you don't want to say.

DIALOGUE 2

Reaching the Prospect

YOU: *"How are you today? My name is John Smith and ... uhm ... I'm with XYZ Investments and I ... ahh ... wanted to see if you might have time for a cup of coffee and to hear about the ... uhm ... incredible results we've been producing for our clients."*

What went wrong:

- When you ask, *"How are you today?"* the person answers hesitantly because they're naturally suspicious and listening only for a reason to stay on or get off the call.
- When you state your name, they try to think of all the people they know with your name, which confuses them. If you have a name like Sarano then they're definitely confused. I've had prospects refer to me as "Saranomo," "Geranimo," and "whatever your name is."
- The minute you tell them your firm's name, their suspicion that this is a cold call is confirmed. They stop listening and wait for you to take a breath so they can say, "I'm not inter-

ested" or "I already have an advisor."

- The word "might" is about as powerful as "I was wondering." Most people are way too busy for "might" and "wonder."
- "Time for a cup of coffee"… Seriously? What is the likelihood that a busy person has nothing better to do than go to coffee with somebody who cold calls them?

Before you tell me you don't sound like that cold caller above, my question is, have you ever recorded one of your phone conversations? (Check with compliance and your state's recording laws first.) Have you ever had anyone count the number of times you say "uhm" or "ah"? This can be eye opening.

We want you to understand the rules of communication because there are times we'll follow them and times when we'll suspend them. What I mean is, you will structure your dialogue in a way that causes the person to listen because you will know what they're listening for.

Here's how the conversation should flow:

- Begin by saying the prospect's name. Hearing their name will grab their attention.
- After saying their name, say *"listen."* In most cases they're only half-listening and trying to decide if they should fully listen to you.
- To further connect with them, try mirroring what they may be thinking by saying something like: *"We haven't spoken,"* or *"We haven't met yet,"* or *"I know you weren't expecting my call."*
- Go immediately to a "headline" or the most compelling part of your message. Do not save this until the end. That is bad strategy because they may not keep listening that long. You want to go with your strongest hand first.
- Go to your message. Once you have gained their interest

with a headline, you must make sure you have a compelling message.

- End with a reason why they should meet with you now — express some form of urgency. Don't give them a reason to put you off.
- Make sure you include your name and your firm's name.

DIALOGUE 3

The Right Formula

Here's how you can put it all together. I am playing the role of the advisor:

"Joe, listen, I know you weren't expecting my call and we haven't met yet. I'm concerned about how a lot of your clients could react to a serious decline in the markets, and while you're busy advising them, my question is, who's advising you? As a leading communications trainer and top speaker for our industry, I want to help you get out in front of this potential situation and go over a unique and timely strategy. I'll be in town next week on Wednesday and Thursday -- which of those two days can we meet? My name is Sarano Kelley and I'm a co-founder of The Kelley Group."

The cold-calling scripts that Brooke and I have written for our coaching clients all follow the rules cited above. However, each one is proprietary to a specific advisor and based on their unique value proposition. They are all approved by a respective firm's compliance department to ensure they stay within their guidelines.

Of course, even if you follow the script perfectly, chances are that 90 percent of the prospects will let you know that they're not interested. However, this is not an outright "no." If they meant "no," they would likely say "no." Anything other than a "no" is an objection.

We will use the same process for handling objections that was discussed in the previous chapter, but we want to emphasize that because this is a cold call, you're only looking to secure a meeting with the prospect. The process (without the actual dialogue) is as follows:

Prospect: Objects (to meeting)

YOU: Replay

Prospect: Verifies

YOU: Acknowledge, Reframe and make the request for a meeting again

Prospect: Objects (again)

YOU: Replay

Prospect: Verifies

YOU: Acknowledge, Reframe and make the request for a meeting again

This continues until you both negotiate a meeting or reach a standstill. At this point you would engage in a "walk away" by saying something like:

"I want to thank you for your time and consideration. I enjoyed our conversation (this should be true). *May I get you some literature?"*

Most people will say "yes." This is the point where a cold call could migrate into the next level of strategy because research shows that most people don't say "yes" until they have given seven "nos" or had seven opportunities to consider your offer.

If you're making calls to people who are in your area, you can make plans to drop off the literature to them. The scenario then changes from cold calling to warm walking. You can then say to the receptionist or assistant:

"Joe and I were on the phone earlier this week and I promised him that I would get some information over to him. I'm in the area seeing clients and am in a bit of rush, but if he has five minutes I'd be glad to shake his hand and put a face with a name."

What happens next will depend on further strategies discussed in this book. The main thing is, you've moved the ball down the field. Now you can work on getting further touch points with this person and gain leverage. This is a game of infinite moves.

The Evolution

Remember when I first attempted to cold call Steven Spielberg, and it was an abysmal failure? Surprisingly, it was the same skill — cold calling — that enabled me to contact a foundation and reignite my mission to reach him. Learning to increase my pace, get into the zone and reframe objections all led to the many successes in my life. And I have my foundation in cold calling to thank for it.

As this process continues you will see that each strategy builds on the one prior, like the way cold calling can lead to "warm walking" which could have you move to connecting with the same person on Linkedin. From Linkedin you can could move to the kind of social networking events your prospects would be a part of and so on and so forth up the scale until you're so well-known they're calling you.

❖❖❖

Reversing the Deal Flow

CHAPTER 4

STEP 2

Walking Up to a Stranger
Starting a Productive Conversation

We've all programmed our children to watch out for "stranger danger" and not to converse with someone they don't know. But you shouldn't feel that way as an adult — particularly if you are a financial advisor. You need to shed the fear of talking to strangers and learn how to start a productive dialogue. In fact, once you've done it several times, the feelings of dread and anxiety should rapidly dissolve. However, it's important to know how to start a dialogue that will head you in the right direction.

This strategy in the Reversing the Deal Flow process will serve you well in mastering the higher rungs in the process. For example, as you build your network you'll often find yourself involved with charitable, civic, religious, political, sports and entertainment events where you have to meet and mingle with strangers. Knowing how to

Brooke's Notes

If you're training for the Olympics, your coach is rarely interested in your opinion on the difficulty of the training or how many yards you must go. In fact, the way to be handed a tougher workout is to question the one you were given. Sarano and I aren't that punishing with our clients, but we do hold fast to one rule: You are to follow the scripted dialogue our way until you can recite it in your sleep. Only then can you try it your way. Long term, this is a program that is about statistics, and you will ultimately use the version that gets you the highest statistical returns.

All coaches push their team members to attain higher levels. Sarano and I say that you are free to be better than the both of us, but you're not allowed to perform below our level on the exercises we give you.

talk to them will also serve you well when you conduct your own "campaigns" or special events. The more strategy steps you master, including this one, the more useful you become to others. People will want to include you in their efforts because it advances their goals and objectives.

Don't wait until you reach the top of the scale to say, "Now I'll practice this strategy." The key to the process is that each strategy is a step, and within each strategy there are additional steps. The good news is, you can get results by following the steps with frequency and intensity. The hard part is, you have to take them in a disciplined order.

Steps and Purpose of the Dialogue

Before jumping into the dialogue below, you need a good understanding of the steps involved and the purpose behind the conversation. What is the goal of starting a conversation with a stranger? To get a client? No. To impress them? No. To get them to like you? No. The goal is to conduct a conversation that gets them interested and excited about meeting with you further, with the desired outcome being an actual meeting to hear about your practice and expertise.

To achieve that outcome, the two steps that matter the most are:

1. Bonding with the person, and
2. Finding out what the greatest weakness is in their current investment relationship.

This is not an exercise in being charming, smart, intelligent, and impressive. In many cases, artificial attempts to display these qualities will backfire, and you'll come across as self-important and self-absorbed. The point of having a process is to free yourself, or as Morpheus says in *The Matrix*: "I'm trying to free your mind, Neo. But I can only show you the door." We need you to be interested in others, not try to be interesting.

To execute on the two steps, which are the centerpiece of this dialogue, you need to ask the right questions. For example:

To bond, ask them to share something that is emotional and personal to them. The key question to ask is, *"What makes you passionate about what you do?"* You must then listen intently and take a genuine interest. Faking it doesn't cut it. They must feel that you really care.

To find out what they think is probably the greatest weakness of their current investment relationship, you will ask, *"What do you wish you could most improve about your relationship with the people you currently work with in my field?"*

Make sure you discuss only that topic and don't digress to talking about the economy, politics, or the market. Instead you only want to talk about the relationship, because your goal is to have them consider changing that relationship. The dialogue is intended to establish rapport with them, let them know you are interested in them, and lead to an opportunity to meet and talk with them further.

The challenge in this process is that you must have enough emo-

Brooke's Notes

Our "90-Day Game" coaching program is designed to put you in the "zone." In our coaching program, you are paired up with a total stranger who becomes your "daily accountability partner." Some people think, "OK, I can tolerate this for 90 days." But when we see them five, 10, 15, 20, 25 years later, they tell us they are still in touch with their accountability partner to this day.

You'll likely find the same happens with you and your partner. Although you start as strangers, your relationship can evolve into a lifelong, meaningful bond — and this isn't even part of the program. For me, bringing great people together to do great things is what I'm most passionate about.

tional maturity and character to understand and care about people at a very deep level. You also must know how to remain attentive and how to fight inner distractions. You want to reach that "zone" that unifies the archer, the bow, the arrow and the target. Brooke refers to it as that place where the dance and the dancer become one. People will sense it if you're just going through the motions to get to your desired outcome.

Meeting a Stranger

In our training programs and keynote addresses, we begin with a benchmark exercise. (There has to be a before and after for you to understand the power of the improvements you're making when we train you.) The two-day training program opens with an exercise in which Brooke plays the role of a stranger standing in the front of the room looking thoughtfully at a painting. We then film each advisor as they walk up and start a conversation with her, without coming across as weird, a stalker or a salesperson. In this scenario, you (the advisor) are invited to an art gallery opening. You see a person looking at a painting. How would you approach that person to start a conversation?

The typical mistake many people make when they walk up to someone is to start with a statement that is an evaluation. For example, they might say: "Hey, this is a great party. Isn't it?" or "Wow, that's a really intense painting," or "Wow, I really like that painting," or "Hey, I love the hat you're wearing."

You may assume that because your comments are a positive evaluation or a compliment, there is no harm in saying them. You are mistaken. First, the person can tell that you've been evaluating them, and such comments are not only a little bit creepy, but they can backfire.

DIALOGUE 1

The Wrong Way

> YOU: *"Hey, you know I really love that painting. It's just so beautiful."*

> Stranger: *"Personally, I don't like it."*

That didn't get you off on the right foot, did it? What happens in any evaluation is that you can be incorrect, and people tend to be suspicious of compliments. They know that compliments are a thinly veiled attempt to manipulate. What would be a better way of opening a dialogue?

Starting a Conversation with a Stranger the Right Way

We recommend using a phrase such as:
"What do you think?"

You'll notice that is not an evaluation. There's very little danger in making such a statement. The typical phraseology to use when someone is looking at something is:

"I couldn't help but notice that you were looking at that painting. What do you think of it?"

Even the use of the phrase "I couldn't help" is intentional. It is also accurate because as an observer how could you not wonder what someone is thinking when the art is valued at $100 millions?

What you say is kept strictly to what is observable and in no way represents an evaluation. By speaking about what they are looking at, rather than interrupting their attention or thinking process, you're joining in. To do it any other way, you might be considered a potential distraction, and it's a short runway from that to being a nuisance or pest.

If a person is standing alone at a social event, he or she might feel awkward. Everybody else is talking in clusters, but this person's all alone. You know this person might be someone you should connect with, but you also feel awkward walking across the room and going up to him or her. In this case, you could open that dialogue by saying:

"I couldn't help but notice that you were standing here alone."

Again, instead of making an evaluation, you're making an objective observation. This is an important distinction and a skill that down the road can help you in so many ways. It's your ability to acknowledge what's there — not your interpretation, not your evaluation, but what's so. It's actually the best way to start a conversation.

If you heard two people talking loudly about a sports team, you could walk up to them and say:

"I couldn't help but overhear that you were talking about (name team)."

Your comments correspond to their discussion, so they are easily accepted. They don't cause a lot of dissonance. The phrase *"I couldn't help"* also communicates that this interaction was not necessarily of your own volition. It's as if you were summoned by the occasion. No one can really take offense at that.

Develop some comfort with simple openings such as:

"I couldn't help but notice."

"I couldn't help but see."

"I couldn't help but overhear."

DIALOGUE 2

The Right Way

Let's go over the right way to conduct this conversation as we return to the scenario at the art gallery. I'll be playing the part of the advisor and Brooke will play the part of the prospect:

Sarano: (walks up to a stranger, in this case, Brooke) *"I couldn't help but notice that you were looking at that painting. What do you think of it?"* (conversation starter)

Brooke: *"I'm not really sure what I think of it, but it definitely gets your attention."*

Sarano: *"I'm curious, why did you come to this opening tonight? Are you already familiar with the artist?"* (probe)

Brooke: *"Actually some friends of mine invited me."*

Sarano: (extend your hand as you say) *"My apologies for being so impolite; I didn't even introduce myself. My name is Sarano Kelley. I'm named after a village in Italy though sometimes people know the name from the Serrano chili pepper. And your name is?"* (Introduce yourself and make your name memorable.)

Brooke: *"It's Brooke."*

Sarano: *"Brooke, it's a pleasure meeting you. I don't know many people here and appreciate being invited. If you don't mind me asking, what do you do for a living that has you here this evening? Are you involved in the arts?"* (Use their name right away so you don't forget it, and then probe.)

Brooke: *"Oh I'm not really from the arts world, I'm a business owner. I own a construction company."*

Sarano: *"I have some incredible clients and friends in the construction field. I'm always curious as to what makes people passionate about what they do. What attracted you to your field?"* (elicit positive emotional information)

Brooke: *"My father was in the business and I grew up in it. He was one of the hardest working guys you've ever met. One day he fell ill while I was in college. I left school to help him with the business and never left. We were fortunate and caught the market at a great time for our kind of work and ended up creating a niche for ourselves."*

Sarano: *"Sounds like your dad was fortunate to have you step in and assist him and that you came in at a great time in the market place."*(replay)

Brooke: *"Yeah, we've been fortunate."*

Sarano: *"Congratulations on turning some pretty serious difficulties into a great success story.* (acknowledgement) *I'm curious, what do you love most about what you do?"* (elicit positive emotional information)

Brooke: *"The people. We have a few hundred employees, and they are like my dad — some of the hardest-working people you'll ever meet. My dad did an amazing job of creating a culture that reflects his values."*

Sarano: *"Sounds like the values of your dad and your team really do align. I can see why that would make for a great environment. Not all businesses are so fortunate.* (replay/acknowledgement) *Can I share with you what I do? It's not related to art, but it's something that I love."*

Let's review the five steps learned in the previous dialogue and that you need to follow:

1. Open the dialogue and start a conversation
2. Conduct the dialogue in such a way that they do most of the talking and you are largely listening
3. Introduce yourself and make your name memorable
4. Ask them what they do for a living
5. Ask them why they're passionate about what they do

The next two step take place in the following dialogue:

6. Tell them what you do for a living
7. Tell them why you're passionate about what you do for a living

All of the steps above are about bonding with someone. Think about a time you were at an event, the airport or a bar, and someone poured their heart out to you and you just listened. At the end of the conversation, they felt like you were the greatest conversationalist in the world, yet you barely said a word. This is bonding at its best: You are someone that others feel they can trust enough to share themselves, disclose themselves, be themselves.

Let's continue with steps 6 and 7:

Brooke: *"Sure."*

Sarano: *"My wife and I are business partners. We run a boutique communications company and have the honor of coaching the leadership of the financial services industry and their elite financial advisors in the U.S. and Canada. We have a unique role in the business since we're both coaches and trainers. We coach peak performance and train in marketing, communication and presentation skills."*

(This is where you insert your well-worded "value proposition.")

Sarano: *"The reason we're so passionate about this business is that we're both athletes and educators so we can relate to high performers. In my case, I had a very successful start as an advisor and then at the end of my first year in the business, four children in my extended family died tragically in a fire. I realized from that experience that my purpose in life is to coach people to access their full potential, which is what my wife and I do for the industry we love."*

This last part is where you insert your thoughtful explanation of why you do what you do — not the cerebral answer, but the one that comes from your gut. I have never met a billionaire who, within the first 10 minutes of the conversation, didn't tell me about how poor he was when he started and how hard he had to work to get to where he is today. They are some of the most inspiring people I've ever met. I get the same kind of stories from many of the large producers I meet.

You need to dig a little deeper and tell a story from your life that would give a stranger insight into your motives, your character, your ethics and why you do what you do. If you're honest with yourself and others, there should be a feeling of connectivity between you and the other person. Let's continue:

Sarano: *I know a lot of people in your position have business coaches. I'm curious, what do you like most about the coaches you work with in my line of work? I'm always interested in how our industry is perceived by thoughtful individuals like you."*

Brooke: (talks about the positives)

You then replay, verify, and acknowledge them. Show your real character by saying you're happy for people like her who have a good experience.

Sarano: *"I'm curious, no one is perfect, what do you wish the folks you work with could improve on?"*

This is where you find out how well you did in bonding with the person. Do they feel they can talk to you? Can they openly and honestly share with you what they don't like about their current relationship with their financial advisor?

Brooke: (responds with her answer to the question of "What do you wish could be improved about your current relationship?")

Sarano: Replay, Verify, Acknowledge, and then say, *"I very much enjoyed our dialogue and appreciate your insights about my industry. I'd welcome the opportunity to have a cup of coffee with you and learn more about your goals and objectives. Who knows, maybe I can provide value to you the way you did by sharing with me. I enjoy meeting great people. Do you have a card? Here's mine."*

Following the above steps in order and perfecting the script sequence will give you the confidence to walk up to a stranger and start a productive conversation in nearly any situation. These friendly interactions will help you grow your network and your client base, keeping you on track to reverse the deal flow.

◆◆◆

Reversing the Deal Flow

CHAPTER 5

STEP 3

LinkedIn

Using Scripts to Accelerate Referrals

In recent years, social media has become a powerful way for financial advisors to uncover valuable connections and lucrative referrals. In fact, the percentage of advisors reporting success in gaining clients via social media has grown from 49% in 2013, to 80% in 2016, according to an industry study. [1]

LinkedIn continues to be the most popular social media platform used by financial advisors, and it presents a trove of opportunities for advisors looking to reverse the deal flow. In this book, our focus is on conversational marketing, so we won't get involved in how to create a profile and brand on LinkedIn. Instead we'll focus on the way advisors can use their voice — conversational marketing — to mine the deep veins of LinkedIn for referrals. We'll also show you

---

1 https://www.putnam.com/literature/pdf/EO288.pdf

how to create a standardized approach for connecting with potential referral sources.

Connecting on LinkedIn

First, you want to put in place a standard practice for how you respond when someone reaches out to you on LinkedIn. We suggest that you do not immediately accept their LinkedIn request; instead look them up via an Internet search and then call them. If you start out by accepting the request, you will close out that particular cycle, no personal interactions will have taken place, and you will move on and so will that person.

What you want to do is reach out to that person and have a conversation. When doing this, it's important to have a process. For example, you could establish a personal rule that you will call that person within 24 hours of receiving their LinkedIn request. This keeps the encounter fresh on your mind and likely fresh on their mind. You could also establish a consequence for yourself like we do in our coaching program called "The Game."[2] For instance, you must report the LinkedIn request to your assistant, and if you don't respond within 24 hours, you must buy Starbucks for your entire team that day and over coffee explain why you failed to get this done so they can better support you. This way you provide structure and accountability to your system.

Now, that the procedures have been established, we can move on to the script or dialogue. Let's go over some examples that have been discussed during our coaching sessions on this subject.

---

2 *The Game: Winning Your Life in 90 Days*; © 2011, The Kelley Group Int'l; Sarano Kelley

DIALOGUE 1

Basic LinkedIn "Mutual Benefit" Dialogue

YOU: *"Jane, (start with the person's name) you sent me a LinkedIn request to connect yesterday."*

Go immediately to the leverage that reminds them of who you are and why they would want to talk to you.

YOU: *"This is [your name]. I wanted to personally call you and thank you for your LinkedIn request."* (Acknowledgement) *"It's a pleasure to get a chance to connect with you. Your LinkedIn request definitely brought up some mutually beneficial* (the "hook" or "WIFM") *thoughts for me and I'd like to share them with you. I was wondering if you had a few minutes to speak right now?"*

Jane: *"Oh yeah, definitely, you caught me at a good time."*

YOU: *"Thanks for taking the time. I wanted to tell you that I've made it a personal practice to make sure the people that I link in with are individuals that know me and know that I'm more than glad to introduce them to relationships that are right for them. Obviously, I'd need to know more about them to be able to do that. Also I prefer to have a conversation with them to see why they wanted to link in with me. What was on your mind?"* (Discovery)

Jane responds; you repeat Jane's response, acknowledging her.

YOU: (Make a recommendation/request) *"I would find it very beneficial to establish a mutual agreement with you for referring each other to appropriate individuals in our respective networks on LinkedIn. I just wanted to check and see what your thoughts are on that subject."*

You have now cued up the subject rather than using a direct request or some sort of demand. What you're doing is prompting the other person to address the subject. This will give you an understanding of their willingness to have a mutually beneficial relationship.

DIALOGUE 2

More LinkedIn "Mutual Benefit" Dialogue

YOU: *"Hello, Jane, this is [your name]. Is this a good time, do you have a minute?"*

Notice that this opening assumes that the person is very familiar with you already.

Jane: *"Oh yeah, definitely."*

YOU: *"I want to thank you for reaching out to me through LinkedIn, and your request for us to connect got me thinking. I'd like to connect with you to discuss some of the joint opportunities we may have between us through LinkedIn. Are you interested in doing this?"*

Jane: *"Yes. Yes, I am."*

YOU: *"So, I was excited to see that you found me on LinkedIn. Can you tell me why you decided to connect with me? What was on your mind?"*

Notice how we suggested you ask a question that will unearth what the person was thinking when they initiated the LinkedIn request. That way you know how to address that person and continue the dialogue. Also, you'll know up front whether or not that person is a fit for your practice.

In addition, you'll want to give the conversation context and direction. They can then begin to talk about what was on their mind so you have more information about the person and the situation you're dealing with.

It is entirely possible that a person might say, *"Yeah, that's great, let me tell you what I was thinking."* And what could emerge is a very constructive, collaborative dialogue about how they would be glad to refer you, and then you know that you'd be glad to refer them. From there, you can decide whether you should do something about asking for introductions now or simply secure their commitment to refer you in the future. The determining factor will be your current level of lead flow. You could do something now or you could also decide to schedule something for the future. What we want to avoid, of course, is the problem of having more leads than you can and will follow up on. Believe it or not, this does happen more often than many people would want to admit.

The next step might be to tell the person:

"Hey, I really would

Brooke's Notes

In the Reversing the Deal Flow process, we're looking for a portfolio approach to marketing the business. We're not looking for the silver bullet. Right? It's a mistake to stake your professional services practice on a silver bullet. The good news is, you're in the financial services world so you understand the need for diversification as a way to manage risk.

You could think of this as simple diversification, but actually it's more like compound interest. The earlier levels and forms of marketing create a base for the later forms. It is a "layering" in of various marketing approaches where ultimately the whole is greater than the sum of the parts. Once you do that, it is entirely possible that you will arrive at a single action that will look to others like it was a "silver bullet," when in fact it will be "the straw that breaks the camel's back." Unfortunately, when presenting my marketing program to advisors, I find a lot of them are only competent in one strategy, and by coincidence that strategy just happens to be "the silver bullet."

like to discuss the possibility of you and me getting together and maybe doing a deeper dive. Perhaps we could meet and review each other's LinkedIn profiles to see if there are some meaningful opportunities for each of us."

On the other hand, you could come up against someone who hesitates or rejects your offer.

DIALOGUE 3

Handling LinkedIn Partnering Rejection

Jane: *"Look, I'm not someone who would do that given the confidentiality of my business and my relationships."*

YOU: *"It sounds like you're saying you're not very comfortable with that."* (Replay)

Jane: *"Yes, that's what I'm saying."* (Verify)

YOU: *"I want to thank you for being up front."* (Acknowledgement) *"I'm a little confused though, what were you thinking when you reached out to me? What were you hoping would occur?"* (Reframe)

This line of questioning will help you determine if the person is just trying to increase his/her list of connections and was not committed to engaging in networking. In this case, you could summarize what they said:

YOU: *"So you were just looking to increase the number of people in your network, but it wasn't your intention to share appropriate contacts with each other?"* (Summarization)

Jane: *"Yes"*

YOU: *"I see. Well, I'll be glad to accept the request and I want to thank you for being up front with me. If anything changes about that, definitely give me a call and let me know if I can be of assistance to you in the future. Thanks for wanting to include me in your Linkedin network."* (The "walk away")

End of conversation.

What happens when you run into a situation in which the person falls into a "maybe" category? For instance, the person says: "Well, now is not a good time for me to actually introduce you to people. I'm in the middle of some major projects," or "I'm not really comfortable doing that." This is not a "no" answer, it is a "maybe." Remember that you want to anticipate responses so you know how to direct the flow of the conversation.

DIALOGUE 4

Handling LinkedIn Mutual Benefit Objection

YOU: *"I'd really like to discuss the potential for us to get together, maybe do a deeper dive to see if we can meet and review each other's LinkedIn profiles and see if there really are some meaningful opportunities for each of us."*

Jane: *"No, I'm not comfortable with that."*

YOU: *"OK, it sounds like that's not something you're comfortable with.* (Replay)

Jane: *"Right."* (Verification)

YOU: *"Well, Jane, I would never want you to do anything that's uncomfortable for you, and I really want to thank you for being up front with me about that.* (Acknowledgement) *You know, Jane, I'm always looking to learn from people like you, and perhaps that's something I should be concerned about. I'm just curious, what is it about introducing people from your LinkedIn network that is uncomfortable for you?"* (Reframe)

Jane: *"I think I just want to get to know you a little bit better be-*

fore I introduce other people to you."

See how the conversation above moved from handling a "change this person's mind" situation to more of a negotiation. The negotiation is, how much more does the person need to know about you to feel comfortable? In this instance, you wouldn't try to change this person's mind. That would be like taking them hostage, when what you really want from them is willingness. In this case, you choose to use reframing to negotiate a mutually satisfying outcome.

YOU: *If you were me, how would you go about getting you more comfortable?* (Reframe to gain specificity)

Remember, you don't want to waste time and energy on someone who isn't interested in working with you. You want them to tell you what and how much they need to know. This would be one way of handling an objection. If what they want and need to become comfortable is more than what is prudent for you, then this would go from an objection to a negotiation to a "walk away" scenario.

You don't want to presume that everyone who wants to connect with you on LinkedIn will want to take the relationship further. In other words, they say "yes." Much of what you'll face won't be a "yes" or "no," it will be a "maybe." And as we've discussed in this book, maybes are objections, and objections are a form of consideration. By consideration, we mean that the person has issues, concerns and perhaps even misinformation that must be clarified and or corrected for the relationship to move forward. Your job is to help them sort out that consideration and to get them to respond with either a "yes" or a "no." If you get them to a "no," great, it's a walk away. If you get them to a "yes," that's awesome. But do not leave them at a "maybe."

Is It Worth Your While?

In some cases, you may wonder whether a LinkedIn invitation is worth your time to pursue. In this case, you might have an intern or a marketing or sales assistant make the call and say:

DIALOGUE 5

Having an Assistant Follow Up on LinkedIn Request

Assistant: *"(Your name) noticed that you were looking to link in with him, and he was excited to make contact with you. He asked me to reach out to you to schedule an opportunity to speak. I'd like to schedule that. Before I do, I just want to check with you, was there a particular purpose that you had in linking in with Joe?"*

The person will answer. The assistant will replay. The person will verify. The assistant will acknowledge the person and say, *"I'm just curious, what were you looking to achieve?"*

If the person's response is something that would not be beneficial to your practice, the assistant could say:

Assistant: *"I really want to thank you for the inquiry, but I also don't want to waste your time. At this time, that would not be a fit for us, but now that I know more, I can certainly brief Joe and keep that in mind for the future. And I would be delighted to do so."*

An assistant or intern who is good at screening calls and has a well-designed script can save you energy and time. The goal is to be able to screen opportunities and to pass them through the process quickly. If they're a fit, great. If they're not, move on.

There is also a reverse scenario to consider with LinkedIn. That is, if you are sending out invites and someone accepts, you call them and say:

DIALOGUE 6

When You Send Out a LinkedIn Invitation

YOU: *"This is Joe Jones, and I noticed you accepted my LinkedIn invitation. It brought a great idea to mind that I wanted to run by you. Do you have a quick moment?"*

The reason to use the words "quick moment" is because it's easy for a person to say, *"No, I don't have time."* We say it brought a great idea to mind so that you give them something to be interested in, even if the interest is mysterious at the outset. If you just ask people if they have time and you give them no reason to say "yes," they will find it easier to say "no."

YOU: *"I notice from your LinkedIn profile and the people that you're connected to, there might be some synergies between the two of us from a business point of view. I was wondering if you had any thoughts in mind when you accepted my LinkedIn invitation."*

This scenario has the same elements of dialogue as the previous scripts. The mistake people make with LinkedIn is to presume that sending and receiving invitations will automatically lead to referrals. It may and it may not. But making a plan to follow up on invitations, formulating a presentation, and adhering to a process will significantly increase your success rate. There is nothing wrong with using social media for brand awareness, but I don't suggest you think of it as marketing nor should you expect the same kind of results you can get from direct marketing.

Think of your LinkedIn profile as a billboard, as brand awareness and as a very passive strategy. When you direct your LinkedIn invitations and actions to a specific target with the intent of following up, that's what we consider direct marketing. When you call the person and make an actual request, that's what we call selling. These three disciplines work best together (and many attempted strategies have failed because the advisor only used one or two out of the three).

Another question the advisors we coach often ask is whether it's beneficial to accept LinkedIn invitations from a wide swath of people.

While you need to be discerning when you accept invitations, you also want to remember that you're on the site to "get known" and expand your network.

For example, you might get a LinkedIn request from a college student and wonder whether to accept it. You don't recognize the person's name and he or she doesn't seem to fall within your client demographics. Why are they reaching out to you? Consider this: That student could be the son or the daughter of someone who's very successful in the world of business or a potential center of influence (COI) to your practice, and that's how they heard about you. People within the demographic audience you want to reach have various "touch points": family, friends, professional associates, and COIs. You want to be open and available to these connections as well. This doesn't necessarily mean that you, your assistant or business development partner will call all of them; however, if one of you has the time and capacity then perhaps you should "qualify" them.

Have Realistic Expectations

Having a profile on LinkedIn can increase awareness of your brand and that, in itself, may bring you referrals (thought I wouldn't count on it). Sending and accepting requests may also produce some leads, but we promise your numbers will be significantly higher if you call people. You will need to determine what your success rate is, however, because you're the one running the business.

At the end of the day, as your Virtual Chief Marketing Officers, we would like to share exciting, compelling anecdotal stories, but we know you prefer actual assets over stories. Be careful when people tell you incredible marketing stories about their amazing results using LinkedIn. That particular example could be a reflection of "dumb luck" (which is shorthand for a large volume of marketing that leads to incredible success). It's like finding money in the street: It's a great thing to have happen but it's no way to plan on paying your mortgage.

Keeping Stats

As with the other marketing approaches outlined in this book, keeping and monitoring statistics will assist you in evaluating and troubleshooting each strategy. In this case, the statistics could be:

- How many Linkedin requests did you send (last week or month)?
- How many Linkedin requests did you receive (last week or month)?
- How many of those people did you call?
- How many people said "yes" and wanted to move forward?
- How many people said "no" and did not want to move forward?
- How many people were not a fit?
- What specific objections did you encounter?
- Which ones were you most successful reframing or negotiating with?
- Which ones were you least successful with?
- How much business have you come across as a result of Linkedin?
- How much business have you closed based on Linkedin?

◆◆◆

CHAPTER 6

STEP 4

Social Networking

Face-to-Face Communication

People are naturally social creatures, right? So it should be easy to walk into a room and automatically be able to strike up a conversation with anyone there. Not exactly. Interpersonal communication isn't always natural and easy, and the circumstances surrounding a situation or event — the context — plays a big role.

We define social networking in this book as going to an event or gathering with the purpose of socializing with others to develop business relationships. It is a situation in which the context is pre-established and the rules of order are well known; that is, people are there to socialize and build a network. We often find that many people think they're really good at social networking because they have the gift of gab. But if you take a close look at how people react after a conversation with someone who has the "gift" you will find them rolling their eyes in private.

Introvert or Extrovert

Personally, unlike Brooke, I'm an introvert. I was a stutterer and could not speak intelligibly until age 6, and therefore I was not really a social creature. I also did not grow up in a neighborhood with people "of means" who could have a major impact on my business as a financial advisor. For me, cold calling, public speaking, and becoming good at social networking were "learned" skills and not an innate part of my character.

Brooke, on the other hand, amazes me. I've never seen someone who is so genuinely interested in people. I don't know if that's because she's truly a classic extrovert or simply because of the extreme interest she has in people. After a few hours at a social gathering, I'm ready to go home for some "me time" and she is in the corner of a room listening to someone pour his heart out to her. Then again, her mother was a therapist so perhaps some of that is a learned trait as well.

Most likely, the conversation was one-sided.

This type of person has a false sense of what it means to be effective in a social situation. They think it means being the life of the party or the center of attention. They don't understand that the objective of the interaction is to gain assets, and that gaining assets requires them to proceed through a series of steps. They don't understand that one of the first steps to accomplish in a social setting is to arrange a subsequent one-on-one meeting outside of that event. Unfortunately, here's what we see happening with many advisors: They tout their investment expertise, speak about market trends, and wax eloquent about investment opportunities. These advisors fall prey to the notion that the goal of the exercise is to impress people, when in fact, that's usually a turn off.

They're the kind of advisor people want to avoid and no one enjoys talking to. Why are they that way? One of the primary reasons is a lack of training. It doesn't matter whether you think you're good or bad at social networking, or whether you're extroverted or introverted. You need a process that allows you to develop a skill set that will not only enable you to have great conversations with great people, but to achieve a mutually beneficial outcome.

We often say to the advisors we coach, "When you go out to a networking event, do you usually carry new account forms and paperwork on you for people to sign?" Of course, they look at us like that's a totally absurd question. When they say, "No," we ask them: "Then why are you conducting the social networking interaction as if the goal is to have the person knock the appetizers off the table, whip out a pen, and start signing new account forms because of the genius you portrayed?" I imagine some people get our sense of humor, and I'm also sure that some people are slightly irritated, but they get the point nevertheless.

When engaging in sales at a social networking event, envision the steps on a gradient scale as:

- Get someone's attention
- Gain their interest
- Engage in dialogue
- Have them experience you as interested in them
- Have them come to like you (the key to this is the step above)
- Have them want to know more about you
- Have them be open to a further dialogue with you
- Agree to meet at a later date to learn more about each other

If we kept drawing the steps of the scale straight through the well-documented and detailed steps as they appear in our face-to-face sales program, it would end with:

- Have them move their assets over to you to manage
- Have them feel good about leaving previous advisors with whom they have worked for many years

Looked at metaphorically, if you're single, you wouldn't walk up to a person you're attracted to and say: "I know we don't know each other, but I want you to know I'm going to marry you, and we're going to raise a family together."

Poor Conversation Starters

In the scenarios we discuss in this chapter, you are the person initiating the conversation. Could you be in social networking situations where the other person initiates the conversation? Absolutely. But that's the easier case. When Brooke and I prepare people for intense media interviews, we don't give them the easiest scenario, we give them the most difficult. As Brooke often says, "For training to be real training, it's got to be harder than real life."

More often than not, when people walk up to start a conversation they begin with flattery. Right away, the other person wonders, "What are you up to?" This happens even when you offer a sincere compliment or good evaluation, such as, "I love that tie," or, "That's a lovely dress." It immediately puts that person on the defensive before they have a chance to experience who you really are.

Another big mistake people make is falling into what we call "the trap," which is trying to be interesting rather than being interested in others. Think about a dialogue you've watched or engaged in. Who was doing most of the talking? What was the primary subject of the actual conversation? Whenever you find someone to be obnoxious or imposing, you'll probably notice that individual is doing most of the talking, which of course is an index as to how self-absorbed they are... and they're probably talking mostly about themselves. The odd thing is that the more self-absorbed and the more self-important someone thinks they are, the more insecure they are. This is not the way that you want to portray yourself.

At the same time, you must realize that most people don't mean to come across this way. I doubt they say to themselves, "Let me see how many people I can annoy by being incredibly self-absorbed and by making sure I get my feelings of self-importance across to them." This type of behavior is unconscious and outside of a person's control, and on a bad day we're all likely guilty of it to some degree.

Better Conversation Starters

So what's the right way to start a dialogue? Let's start with one of our more ubiquitous conversation starters, the phrase: *"I'm curious."* Remember, "I'm curious" is a shorthand way of telling the person that you aren't going to give them a reason, rationalization or a long explanation, which can create fear, concern or resistance.

"I'm curious" is then followed by what we call situational interest questions. These are simply ways to productively start a conversation. These questions can be as basic as:

"What brought you here?"

"How are you finding this event?"

"Why have you decided to come?"

"What do you like most about the evening so far?"

"How did you find out about this event tonight?"

"What were you hoping to gain by coming here?"

You'll notice these questions are open-ended, which gives the person a lot of room to respond to your question.

There are no doubt many other situational questions you can use, but remember that our coaching rule is to first teach you how to do things our way and then encourage you to do better.

The wrong way to approach a conversation, of course, would be to talk about yourself: What brought *you* here, how *you're* finding the event, why *you* decided to come, and so on. It's me, me, me. I'm reminded of Bette Midler's quote in the movie *Beaches*: "But enough about me, let's talk about you... what do you think of me?"

The next step in the conversation process is to wait for the individual to respond. Your No. 1 job is to listen, which means not spending your mental energy thinking of witty or related items you might want to bring up to this person. This takes your mind off track. Instead, you need to listen so well that you can recite what the person has said. You need this information to replay, verify and acknowledge what they said.

You may think no one will notice if you're not listening, but there are some very apparent signs: pupils get really small to block outside impulses, facial muscles become flaccid and there's a change in breathing rate. You have probably been in a conversation with someone who you felt was just waiting for their turn to speak, and listening to you was, at best, a necessary requirement to get to what they wanted to say. It's not a very pleasant situation.

After a person answers your question, you want to use the replay, verification and acknowledgement sequence. In this scenario, we want to draw a distinction between using an acknowledgement and a compliment. Sometimes a person you approach may be slightly stand-offish or need to be warmed up. In this situation you'll want to encourage communication. If they're being communicative, you acknowledge them, right? An acknowledgement would be:

"I'm glad to hear that."

"It's great to know that."

"That's good to hear."

You're simply acknowledging the person's response and creating a greater feeling of affinity between the two of you.

However, if you find the person needs more reinforcement or encouragement to get them to talk more, you need to reward them. By this we mean give them a genuine compliment, such as:

"You know, you have a great sense of humor."

"I appreciate how candid you are. It's refreshing."

"I like how positive you are."

"You have a great way of saying things."

These are all ways of providing positive reinforcement to the person for communicating with you. As simple as it sounds, you will find it requires some practice.

The next step would be:

"Given what you're said/ shared, I'm wondering — what do you do for a living?"

If this hasn't come out already, it will give you a sense of whether or not this is someone who fits your client or center of influence (COI) profile. This may sound a bit mercenary, but it is "social networking" and has a purpose.

From there, they would respond, you would replay, they would verify and you would acknowledge them and/or compli-

Brooke's Notes

A common bad habit is to start thinking about what you can say related to the comments the other person is making and then interject it into the conversation to show how knowledgeable you are.

After people go through our two-day training on face-to-face selling and group presentation skills, they are given hundreds of daily exercises to do with a peer partner. We then ask them to go to an event and count how often in an evening they hear people acknowledging other people in conversation. They are astounded to find very few, if any, are doing this. Of course, they also can't help but notice that the people who do execute on this skill happen to be the people that everyone enjoys talking to.

Brooke's Notes

The Connector

Just because someone isn't a fit for your business or social network profile is no reason to not be every bit as attentive to them. One of the highest levels of "marketer" in the Reversing the Deal Flow system is the Connector. This person is someone we all value because they seem to be an inexhaustible source of resources. In truth, they are largely individuals who are naturally interested in people, talk to people, remember them and know what they need. They can put the right people in touch with each other. In most cases this is a gift, though it can be learned, and there is a lot to learn from such people about human interaction.

ment them based on the degree to which they seem to be open to communicating with you.

Emotional Connectivity Questions

Your next step is to ask questions that encourage emotional connectivity. This is critical because asking someone what they do for a living might be informative, but it doesn't necessarily spark a connection with that person. At the end of the day, your goal is to bond with them.

For example, you can say:

"What makes you so passionate about that?"

"You seem to be really excited about what you do. What do you think makes it so exciting for you?"

"You sound like you have a real sense of purpose around that. Why is that?"

Again, you want that person to share their feelings about their work and what emotionally bonds them to the job, because as they share that with you they begin to bond with you as well.

For now we will purposefully stay away from other emotionally bonding questions like:

"What do you find most frustrating about what you do?"

"What are the biggest threats to your industry?"

"What do you wish you could change about what you do?"

These are indeed bonding questions, but it's usually best to save these for face-to-face sales calls. These questions, while penetrating, may leave a negative aftertaste in a person's mind after the conversation is over. Instead, you want to leave them with a pleasant, enjoyable feeling. In fact, the goal we set for you in communicating with people is the same as our own: to leave people better off for having interacted with you.

The Conscious Communication

After you replay, they verify and you acknowledge what they're passionate about, you can then segue into a similar conversation about what you, as an advisor, do for a living. You can use transition statements like:

"I'd love to share with you what I do for a living."

"May I share with you what I do for a living?"

"What you had to say reminded me what I love about what I do for a living. Can I share a bit about that with you?"

Don't be surprised if they ask what you do for a living even before you ask if you can share that. People often sense when there is an imbalance in giving and receiving. When they feel that you have given them lots of attention, interest and listening, they will often turn to you and say, "You know, I've been talking a lot about myself, forgive me, but what do you do for a living?"

Make sure you share what you "do" and not what you "are." For example, if you ask a doctor what she does for a living, she'll say, "I deliver babies." Or, "I cure cancer." She's described a "doing," not a "being."

Advisors often describe what they do in terms of "being," such as, "I'm a financial advisor; I'm a wealth advisor." These are not "doings." As such, they tend to shut down a conversation or repel a person's natural curiosity to learn more. Even worse, the person on the receiving end of "I'm a wealth advisor" would then categorize and catalog you into their already existing idea of what that means, and that could be a very difficult box for you to get out of. It's important for you to use compelling language. Also, be sure you leave them with the key words you use in your branding. Remember, people won't be able to repeat verbatim anything you said, but they will be left with a clear impression based on certain key words you use. Know what those words are and make sure that you communicate them powerfully.

The Unconscious Communication

From there, you'll move the conversation to unconscious communication, or your own emotional bonding communication, similar to when you asked them: "Why are you so passionate about what you do for a living?" At this time you can use dialogue such as:

"The reason why I'm so passionate about my field is ..."

"What inspires me most about what I do for a living is ..."

"What most touches me or moves me about what I do is ..."

"What inspired me to get into the business was..."

For example, when someone asks me, *"What do you do for a living?"* what I say is, *"Brooke and I have the honor and privilege of being the leading coaches to the nation's top financial advisors and the leadership of the financial services industry in both the U.S. and Canada. The reason I'm so passionate about my field is that I had a very successful start early on in the business. However, after that successful start, I had several children in my extended family die in a tragic house fire, and out of that experience I decided that what I love most is helping people achieve their full potential, which is what I do for the industry that I love."*

The first part of the answer satiates a person's conscious or intellectual interest in the answer to the question, but the second portion is designed to give them a window into what unconsciously drives me. Brooke has an equally compelling life story since we both grew up with very little but were fortunate to have incredible upbringings.

The second part of this dialogue, and your answer to why you're passionate about what you do for a living, should be a story that is:

- true,
- real for you,
- speaks to your motives,
- gives people an insight into your character,
- allows people to get to know you on a more personal level, and
- communicates to them in a way that is consistent with your brand.

Questions that Foster a Follow-up Meeting

Once you've given them time to reflect on what you just said about your work passion, allow them to comment. Next you'll use questions that foster a follow up, such as:

"I'm curious. Who are the kinds of people you work with as clients? Given what I've heard, I'd like to tell people about you."

"How are you growing your business?"

Brooke's Notes

Sarano and I were at a charity event put on by an amazing financial advisor who is truly a great connector. He knew I was a fan of country western music, and he invited us to a private event to hear and meet with one of the great country-western superstars of our time.

It was an event for athletes and celebrities who supported the advisor's campaign for children's charities. We had a conversation with the guest performer that mirrored elements of the dialogue structure described in this chapter. At the end of that interaction, he gave us his personal cellphone number and his email address, and followed up with the comment, "I want you to reach out to me if I can help you. There's nothing you would ever ask me to do that I wouldn't do for you." I was speechless.

I've noticed in our interactions with billionaires and top celebrities that, just like this country singer, they usually share something about themselves that is deeply personal. These individuals are confident enough in who they are that, rather than trying to impress, they are very open, and as a result, truly inspiring.

"I wonder if there's any sort of key resources that you're looking for right now, because I work with and come across great people like you."

It's important to recognize that your reason for following up with them will be even more powerful if it includes a "what's in it for them." This is not to say that all people are selfish and self-absorbed, but you must recognize that everyone is busy, everyone's time is valuable. It's unlikely someone will put a high priority on meeting with you unless you give them a good reason to do so. That reason needs to center on them. You want to describe your value to them.

Once they respond to you, you'll go through the sequence of replaying, verifying, acknowledging and/or complimenting before you approach a clear closing.

Let's see how a conversation might flow if we pull all of the individual elements into a single dialogue.

DIALOGUE 1

A Social Networking Conversation

YOU: *"I'm curious – what brought you to this party?"* (Conversation Starter)

Prospect: *"I'm a friend of the host. We both go to the same gym after work and got to know each other there. Sometimes we run together on the weekends or take in a baseball game."*

YOU: *"Oh, you're a friend of Joe Jones, and you met at the gym?"* (Replay)

Prospect: *"That's right."* (Verification)

YOU: *"Are you in the same line of work as Joe? I'm curious, what do you do for a living?"*

Prospect: *"I work at XYZ Company, which is right around the corner from his office. Joe is now a client."*

YOU: *"It's a fascinating field that you're in, and I've heard of your company before. What do you find most rewarding about your work? What makes you so passionate about it?"* (Emotional Connectivity Question)

Prospect: *"We get to work with really incredible people like Joe, and what we provide changes their lives because we simplify how they run their business, saving them time and money. As a senior partner at my firm I don't just consult with the heads of the major businesses we work with, they think of me as a valued partner and friend, which is how I ended up here this evening."*

This is where you would replay, verify and acknowledge them.

YOU: *"It sounds like you get to provide incredible value and forge some great personal relationships at the same time."* (Replay)

PROSPECT: *"That right."* (Verification)

YOU: *"I admire people who are passionate about what they do for a living, and it says a lot about your relationship that Joe invited you here this evening."* (Acknowledgement) *"I find the same satisfaction in my own work."* (Segue)

This is where you would insert your value proposition. We coach advisors to develop a message that communicates their unique brand. There is no recommended script, but there are recommended guidelines:

- Start with "we" rather than "I." It's more accurate — unless you do everything from investment management to taking out the garbage. It also adds some mystery, which creates interest. When you say "I" you may unintentionally diminish their sense of the scope of your organization.

- Do not say, "I'm a wealth advisor," or "I'm a financial advisor." These bland descriptions make it easy for the person to dismiss you and stop listening.

- Stay away from the word "work." People are not going to remember every word you say. However, they will remember certain words, so you need to choose them wisely. "Work" is not a particularly sexy word from a marketing point of view. More attractive words are: develop, collaborate, build, strategize, partner, etc. My father was a blue-collar worker who truly "worked," and I'm grateful he did. I don't think "work" applies quite as well to advisors.

- Avoid saying "people," as in: "I work with people." Instead, define the type of clients you serve who most resemble the person you're speaking to.

Here's what the opening might sound like:

"We collaborate with top minority entrepreneurs who are great at what they do and focus most of their energy and talents on their own business. They see us as a trusted resource, and we function as a virtual family office managing a wide range of their financial affairs."

A wrong opening is:

"I'm a financial advisor and I work with people on their investments."

After you've shared what you do (Conscious Communication), you can now tell them a personal story that explains why you are passionate about what you do.

YOU: (Continuation) *"The reason I'm so passionate about what I do is that I learned the value of hard work at an early age growing up on a farm. My dad taught me the value of hard work and treating all people fairly, but despite that hard work, my father came close to losing the farm several times. I could see that it had nothing to do with his hard work and everything to do with not having the right circle of financial experts. After I got my MBA, I decided to dedicate my life to providing my clients like Joe with what my dad never had."*

Keep in mind that your story must be true and real — not just the words but the deep conviction and sincerity in your voice and facial expression.

PROSPECT: *"My upbringing was very instrumental in my decisions as well. I work hard, and I have to admit that my life is a lot better because my parents instilled that trait in me."*

YOU: *"I'm curious. Who are the other kinds of people you work with as clients, besides Joe? Given what I've heard, I'd like to tell people about you. If you have a card, I'd welcome the opportunity to get together some time."* (Follow-up Question and Closing)

Closing

The dialogue you use in closing could include one of these options: *"I enjoyed meeting you and I'd like to think about what we discussed and get back together sometime to learn more about you."*

"Some of the things you shared really struck a chord with me, and I would love to connect in the future. May I get your card?"

The best way to get someone to give you his or her card is to simultaneously reach for yours as you ask for theirs. If someone doesn't give you their card, that doesn't necessarily mean anything. However, if someone is standoffish and not really willing to engage with you, in all likelihood this person is not someone that you want as a client or center of influence. As you know, this is a numbers game and there's no reason to take hostages. It would be best to politely end the interaction and walk away.

DIALOGUE 2

Social Networking — Walk Away on Good Terms

"Forgive me if I was a bit too forward. I was impressed by what you had to say and may have been a bit overzealous. I'm sure our paths will cross again since I'm often in situations where I meet great people like you. I wish you the best with your business."

However, if the person is someone you genuinely enjoy and want to get together with, your main goal at this point is to sell them on wanting to see you again, at which point you can move to the next phase of the process. Don't move too quickly until you know their current situation, do discovery, and know their past experiences. The process involves an orderly progression of steps. Like any kind of game or sport, it's much more fun and rewarding when you understand the rules and how the game is played.

Post-Social-Networking Email/Note

Following the social networking event, you want to quickly send the person a follow-up communication. If you have the person's mailing address, it would be even more meaningful to send a hand-written note. In the note or email, you want to:

Repeat something memorable that they said. Avoid writing something clever that you thought up or said. Yes, you can add something meaningful that you said, but remember this is about them, not you. You can talk more about yourself later, once they understand the true value you represent.

- Acknowledge or compliment them on something they said.
- Let them know that you were inspired, moved or touched by something in the conversation, but make sure you are genuine.
- Let them know you'll be reaching out to them to arrange a get-together.

One of the benefits of this process, and one of its tenets, is that we don't want you to do or say anything that isn't true for you. The reason for scripting is to give you structure, and ultimately you will find that structure sets you free — free to create, to generate, to be you at your best. Of course, to get to that point requires the same dedication it takes to get to Carnegie Hall: "practice, practice, practice."

Follow-up Phone Script

Following the event, you will also want to call the person. Just like any warm-calling script, there is a sequence to follow. Most advisors will start with something like: "Hey Bob, it's Jim. I just wanted to call to see how you're doing and catch up. How are things going?" Meanwhile, the person is wondering, "Jim? Jim who? What Jim? Jim from work? Jim from church? Is this Jim from college? Which Jim am I talking to now?" The conversation begins on a confusing and awkward note.

Here is the sequence you want to follow:

1. Start with their name.
2. Remind them of where you met and ideally mention something that connects them back to your conversation.
3. Let them know you've been thinking about the interaction and you'd like to get together.
4. Suggest a time and a place.

Following is a sample dialogue.

DIALOGUE 3

YOU: *"Bob, This is [your name]. I've been thinking about our interaction at Joe Jones' event the other night, and the comment you made about your parents and what you love about what you do definitely struck a chord with me. It just so happens I have time next Thursday, and I was wondering if we might meet?"*

Now, it's possible you may encounter objections. For example:

Bob: *"I appreciate what you're saying, but I really don't have a lot of time."*

YOU: (WRONG) *"Oh really, we don't need a whole lot of time, blah, blah, blah, blah, blah, blah, pitch, pitch, pitch."*

Here is the right way to handle the conversation:
Bob: *"I don't have time."*

YOU: (Replay) *"It sounds like you have a lot on your plate right now."*

Bob: *"Yeah, I do."*

YOU: (Acknowledgement) *"Given what you told me about what you do and how passionate you are about it, I'm not surprised."*

YOU: (Reframe #1) *"If there was a time in the future that might be good for you, when would that be?"* (or Reframe #2) *"If you were me, what would you suggest as a way for us to be able to connect in the future?"*

These are just two options out of many you could use; however, I suggest you start with memorizing these before you decide to add additional arrows to your quiver. Often if you have too many choices, in a moment of awkwardness or discomfort you might find yourself throwing everything at them but the kitchen sink.

Worst Case Scenario

As the often-quoted saying goes: "Hope for the best, plan for the worst." In this case, what do you do if the person blows you off? We have a plan for that — use the skill we refer to as an appropriate emotional response. With this type of response, you don't immediately replay without first acknowledging that there was some emotional content in what a person said.

Let's take an obvious and emotionally charged situation that we all find difficult, the loss of a loved one, to better understand what we mean by an "appropriate emotional response." For example:

Bob: *"Oh you know, I just lost a close friend."*

YOU: (WRONG) *"So, a close a friend of yours just passed away."*

This is indeed an accurate replay, but it lacks any sense of empathy or recognition of what the person is going through, which makes it wrong. The right way is to begin by making a statement that acknowledges what the person is feeling or how you feel about what they must be going through.

YOU: (RIGHT) *"I'm really sorry to hear that. It sounds like you just lost someone important to you and have a lot on your plate right now."*

The appropriate emotional response is important when you hear emotional content, otherwise the person feels like you heard them, but you didn't understand them.

If someone is rude to you or off-putting, you are dealing with a situation that has difficult emotional content (though different from the loss of a loved one) that you must address. In such a case, you'd use an emotional probe rather than an appropriate emotional response. What is the difference between an emotional probe and an emotional response? Some examples of emotional probes are:

"Did I say something that offended you?"

"I feel like I may have somehow offended you."

"I apologize and may have overstepped my boundries. Did you feel like I was being too pushy?"

In some cases, after you bring up their reaction a person may decide they were overreacting and reconsider how they are interacting with you. They may even choose to meet with you despite the fact that things got off on the wrong foot. At the very least, you want them to know you're in tune with their feelings, and you did not intend to offend or upset them. Brooke continually tells our coaching clients that much of what we teach could be summed up as "good manners." Unfortunately, while good manners are just common sense, they're not as common as we would all like to imagine, especially when you're dealing with rude or inconsiderate people.

The Walk Away

What about a situation in which you want to walk away? Even though you may be tempted to stop talking and leave, keep in mind that you don't know who this person knows or who they might be connected to. More importantly, there's no reason to be rude. Generally speaking, no one intends to be rude. However, it can happen when our feelings are hurt, we're embarrassed, or we just don't know what to say to end the dialogue and disengage productively.

In those situations, it's helpful to use phrases such as:

"I apologize if I put a damper on your evening. I thoroughly enjoyed the conversation with you and wish you the best."

"I always like to believe that I leave people better than I met them, and I'm disappointed in myself that our interaction wasn't as satisfying to you as it was for me, but I do wish you the very best."

These dialogues help you to become excellent communicators, and we want you to be goodwill ambassadors in a world where many people struggle to communicate effectively.

Social networking is an important concept in reversing the deal flow because it helps you expand your network of acquaintances and make lasting connections. The larger your network, and the more connections you create, the more you will see referrals flowing back to you. Communication is the clasp that holds the "necklace" of strategies together.

You could view this entire process as building a social network that aligns the right people with your unique and well-known brand so when prospects hear about you, they are calling you and asking to become clients."

◆◆◆

Brooke's Notes

Our coaching clients have experienced some incredible and emotionally moving achievements because of our own social network of great people here at The Kelley Group.

In one case, an advisor with one of the top advisory firms in the industry had a son who was desperately in need of a kidney transplant. Sarano and I organized a 90-day game plan to make that happen, and within 90 days it did. When Sarano saw him not long ago, the advisor proudly showed him a picture of his son and told him how much his son had grown since the transplant.

In another case, which did not end the way we'd hoped, an advisor was dying of a rare liver disease. Within our social network, one of the advisors we coached offered half of his liver to save this young man's life. This advisor and Sarano appeared on a popular television show to share this amazing story of altruism and social connectivity. Unfortunately, despite all of our efforts the young advisor with the liver disease did not survive, leaving behind a wife and young children. However, team members in this advisor's coaching group "adopted" the advisor's widow and trained her on how to run her deceased husband's advisory practice.

In both of these cases the results had nothing to do with us and everything to do with the fact that we are fortunate to have an incredible network of clients who also happen to be some of the most incredible people on the planet. We may be a bit biased, but we believe that we have good reasons to feel that way.

CHAPTER 7

STEP 5

Family, Friends and Social Acquaintances
How to Approach Your Inner Circle

When an advisor is looking for new clients, the easiest and most available group to reach out to is family, friends and close acquaintances. Or so it would seem. But our research shows that the vast majority of advisors shy away from this familiar group for fear of becoming "That Guy."

Who is "That Guy"? In the classic 1993 film *Groundhog Day*, Bill Murray's character Phil Conners runs into a former high school classmate who now sells insurance. He's the stereotypical annoying salesman who says: "Do you have life insurance? Cuz if you do, you could always use a little more. Am I right or am I right, or am I right, right, right, right?" He's the quintessential person that everybody wants to avoid because he's always trying to sell them something.

You've surely been at social situations, clubs, or other places where there was someone who everyone tended to avoid because they were always promoting their own agenda. For many advisors, the fear of being perceived as "That Guy" becomes a phobia, despite the fact that they are competent, skilled advisors who can help their close circle of friends and family.

Advisors who are suffering from this phobia need to view their position in a new light. It's a process of re-alignment. For example, one of our clients (an advisor) is a renowned sports figure who has even competed at the Olympic level. He keeps his athletic "hobby" separate from his business pursuits. In other words, he doesn't talk business to those he has met while engaging in his sports passion. He doesn't want those friends to think of him as "That Guy." As a result, his business is out of alignment with his social life.

Inevitably, when you don't see yourself as "the brand" and the marketing of that brand as something that can be a part of your day-to-day experiences and activities, you'll find yourself in the all-too-familiar spot "between a rock and a hard place." In contrast, we often find that some of the largest producers combine their personal passions with the people they most enjoy working with — those who share their passions. This gives them a highly aligned strategy that reduces the time conflict and removes some of the drag on the enjoyment of one's work.

This is one of the reasons advisors face challenges in balancing their lives: They're juggling situations that ideally should be aligned. They're making the mistake of only branding themselves as a friend, family member or sports buddy, when also they should be branding themselves as valued and preferable resources for providing financial advice. When you're able to work with your friends, family, and social acquaintances, you can spend time with them without feeling like you're sacrificing the business.

It's time to re-brand yourself. Again, these friends, family, and social acquaintances already know you. They already trust you, but they haven't identified you as being their No. 1 choice for handling or managing their money. Do you need to change your script or opening approach for this natural base? Very likely. Our approach is based on both authentic communication and knowing the issues that could arise, and the likely sequence in which they occur. This is important to know, not just for the scripts and dialogue that are provided here, but for the development of your own natural flow of conversation.

How to Initiate a Dialogue

What should be the first words that come out of your mouth? Those first words may not be the most meaningful, but they are the most important because if you don't know how to start a conversation, you probably will avoid that conversation. Brooke often compares this to single guys looking to meet girls: If they don't know how to begin the dialogue, then they spend the evening wishing they would have.

The answer to this issue is simple, and the simplicity is what makes it so powerful. How do you open a dialogue with a friend, family member or social acquaintance? What is your opening line? The relationship is the context for the communication, so your opening is about your relationship.

For example, you might say something like:

"You know, we've been friends ever since college."

"You know, we've been on the same Board together for years."

"You know, our kids have played in the same sports league together for years."

"How long have the two of us been playing golf together?"

Here are some "What if?" situations that you may encounter and some examples of how to structure the referral conversation.

Dialogue With Long-Time Sports Friend

You're at the golf club and everyone else has gone to the bar. You're sitting with someone you've been golfing with for years and have a moment alone. You know you won't be interrupted. This is an opportunity to initiate a conversation about your business.

DIALOGUE 1

YOU: *"Bill, there's something that's been on my mind for a long time and I've had difficulty bringing it up with you."*

Why do you say there's something that's been on your mind for a long time? You've been golfing together for 12 years. What are the odds that they're going to believe that this is the first time you've ever thought about managing their money? Probably not likely, and the last thing that you want to do is come across as disingenuous. Acting as if this is the first time this thought has ever crossed your mind is an obvious mistake; not acknowledging this has been on your mind is a dangerous mistake.

You could even go as far as to say:

YOU: *"The reason I never brought it up is that I value our personal relationship, and I have a hard time bringing up business with friends."*

You are simply anticipating and answering a question you know will be on their mind. Now that you've opened the conversation and admitted that it's been on your mind but that you've been uncomfortable bringing it up, you need to anticipate and answer the next likely question on their mind: "Why have you not brought this up before?" They could be thinking: "Okay, if I've known you for 12 years why are you bringing it up today? Is your business in trouble? Are you desperate? Why now out of any other day over the last 12 years?" You need to answer this question by getting out in front of the issue.

YOU: "I recently began working with a coach. This coach brought something to my attention that I hadn't realized before."

You are providing the true reason that you've chosen this time to talk. The great thing about the truth is that it's easily remembered because there's only one version of it. People are often blown away in our corporate communication skills trainings when they see themselves on tape and we point out how different they look when they're telling the truth versus when they're "making it up as they go" or trying to use some pompous approach (as is the case with many of the scripts I have read that "outside" consultants have tried to sell advisors on).

Also keep in mind that there's nothing wrong with letting people know you have a coach. Many successful people have coaches, and there's nothing unusual about that. People respect individuals who are looking to better themselves.

Next you want to approach the friend with the information that came up during your coaching with us.

YOU: *"Here at the club I have friends who I play golf with and I manage their money. Then there are people here at the club who are friends that I'm very close with, but I don't manage their money. In both cases they're good friends. But what the coach brought up is that if someone like you heard from someone else here at the club that I was managing their money and that I had never brought the subject up with you that it might give you a wrong impression. The coach mentioned that my friends might think that I don't really care about their financial well-being or that I'm not interested in working with them — none of which is true. I just have a difficult time bringing it up. (OR: "I have a hard time bringing this up because I never want to come across as "That Guy." I'm sure you know what I mean by that.") I wanted to have this conversation with you to see what you think."*

Why this approach? If your friend Bill went golfing with a mutual social acquaintance, and that acquaintance happened to mention that you were their advisor and managed their money, then Bill might have come up with his own thoughts regarding why you never talked with him about managing his money. Often those explanations represent their worst fears. Maybe Bill thinks you don't like him. Maybe he thinks that you think he doesn't have enough money. Maybe he thinks you're not as committed to him as you are to other golf friends. This is why in the dialogue, when you say to the person, "The coach brought something to my attention that I hadn't thought of before," you are acknowledging that you can unintentionally offend someone by omission. You can also offend people by not sharing what you do for a living.

Notice that the way this conversation ends is by queuing up the subject — not by making a request other than asking the person to share his reactions to the conversation.

How Not to Say It

Here is how a dialogue sounds when you do it the *wrong way* — on the fly, as is the case for many of the advisors when we videotape them at our trainings.

DIALOGUE 2

YOU: *"Bill, you know, as a successful advisor I manage money for a lot of successful individuals like you. I consider you a friend, and I want you to know that if you ever want a second opinion, if you ever want another set of eyes or ears, or you want someone to review your portfolio, just let me know."* (Sound familiar?)

The response from Bill will likely be: "OK." Then there will be an awkward silence and Bill will say to you, "I wonder what's for lunch?" In other words, the request goes nowhere and produces nothing. The key reason for the dialogue is to get the other person to talk so you know what's on their mind. This wrong-way script does not encourage a friend to talk. It does not allow you to discover their past experiences and current perspectives on the topic of working with a friend like you. It doesn't help you understand their current needs and future goals — things you would want to know before making any sort of a recommendation, including working with you.

Person Won't Work with Friends or Family

It's not unusual for people to say to advisors: "You know, you always complain about being so busy. I thought you didn't want any additional clients." Or you might hear them say, "You know, I didn't bring it up because I thought that maybe you didn't want to talk about work or working with me. You didn't bring it up so I didn't bring it up." Our clients are often floored when they get this kind of a response from a friend, family member or social acquaintance. It happens more than you would like to think.

We have coached many advisors who themselves are either celebrities, well-known religious figures, former athletes as well as financial advisors, and their close relations often assume they already know so many people that they're not looking for clients. One of the saddest cases was one of a struggling advisor whose family name is so well known in the world of business that it would be fair to say it is a household name. Although this particular advisor is connected by birth and name to one of the wealthiest families in our nation, it makes no difference because he doesn't know how to have the conversation. The result is that he is doing a fraction of the business he could be doing although he has all of the access and credibility in the world.

The more frequent examples we run into are when a branch manager or top team hires a person because they're so connected, and then they find themselves at a loss for explaining why the person failed or never lived up to their vaunted potential. When we videotape them in sales simulations, review their presentation skills or confidentially interview people around them in their circle of acquaintances, we find they are either not having the conversation, or even worse, they're just bad at it. As a coach, it's sad to watch talented people fail just because they haven't been trained correctly. But that's also the beauty of the business and its entrepreneurial approach: It's up to you to get the resources you need to achieve the success you deserve in our business.

You may encounter someone in your natural circle who has a hard-and-fast rule about not working with friends, family, and social acquaintances. It could be because they had a bad experience that's unrelated to you or your business.

The way to handle this type of situation is to use our strategy devised for handling any objections. As a reminder, there are three outcomes whenever you make a recommendation to someone. One potential outcome is to change the person's mind (reframe). Another is to negotiate the issue to see if you can come to some sort of an accommodation. The third is to just walk away. If this person has a hard-and-fast rule and it is justified, you could always choose to walk away, but recognize that this person, at a minimum, now knows that you care about them. If their current advisor were to drop the ball, you would be the next person they'd think about contacting. How do you approach a person who's had a bad experience, but you're not sure if it applies to you? How would you know? The answer can be found in the way you handle objections.

DIALOGUE 3

YOU: *"Here at the club I have friends I play golf with and I manage their money. Then there are people here at the club who are friends that I'm very close with, but I don't manage their money. In both cases they're good friends. However, the coach brought up that if you heard from someone at the club that I was managing their money, it might give you a wrong impression because I never brought up the subject with you. He mentioned that you might think I don't care about your financial well-being, or that I'm not interested in working with you — none of which is true. I have a hard time bringing this up, so I wanted to have this conversation with you to see what you think about this subject."*

BILL: *"Well, you know, I really feel uncomfortable. I'm really not comfortable working with friends or family when it comes to managing my money."*

Next you demonstrate an understanding of his response. This is done through replay, or confirming what Bill has said.

YOU: *"Oh, so you've actually given this some thought or had a bad past experience, and you really don't work with friends of yours when it comes to managing your money?"*

BILL: *"Yes."*

Now you acknowledge him. What do you acknowledge him for? For being up front.

YOU: *"Bill, you know I really want to thank you for being up front with me. It was a difficult subject for me to bring up and candidly, the most important thing to me is our relationship. I'm really glad that you feel like you can be candid with me."*

The next step is to respectfully and thoughtfully probe Bill's comment so you can better understand if you should walk away or educate him on why his issue doesn't apply to you … if it doesn't.

YOU: *"If you're not comfortable with it, I certainly don't expect you to consider working with me. However, you've piqued my interest. I'm just curious. It sounds like you might have had a past experience or something that maybe didn't go well. Is that the case?"*

Lo and behold, Bill may reveal to you a past experience that left a bad taste in his mouth. But that experience may be something that could never happen with you, so it's a good idea to bring that to their attention. For example, you might explain that your side of the business is strictly regulated and he never should have had that bad experience and could not possibly experience that with you.

The Walk Away with a Friend, Family or Social Acquaintance

DIALOGUE 4

It's important to have a script when it's best you and the prospect not work together. Here is the dialogue when you need to Walk Away from the situation:

Bill: *"Look, I don't work with friends. It's not what I do."*

YOU: *"So you really have a policy to not work with friends?"* (This is a replay.)

Bill: *"Yes, that's what I'm saying."*

YOU: *"I want to thank you for at least having the conversation with me and being up front with me. I want to be up front with you and make sure you know that I care about you and am glad to be there for you if you need me. The most important thing is not leaving you with a wrong impression based on my discomfort with speaking with friends about business.*

If you have a sense of humor you can end the conversation with a joke and say, *"So you won't hold it against me if I continue to beat you in golf, right?"* The key is to be prepared so that you don't make them feel awkward.

Value Beyond a Client Relationship

Friends, family and social acquaintances don't have to become clients to provide value to your practice. For example, they could:

- Educate you on their industry and the key people in it.
- Provide a reference for you.
- Introduce you to individuals who could be key COIs to you or strategic partners of yours.
- Help you gain entrance to an important club, social circle, group, or association.
- Mentor you. (We'll discuss this successful strategy in Vol. II of the *Reversing the Deal Flow* books.)
- Refer you to people they know who could use your help.
- Bring their friends to an intimate event that you're hosting (as discussed in Vol. II of this series).

When you want to gain their assistance, and becoming a client is not a viable option, you would want to conduct the dialogue like this (as opposed to a Walk Away script):

DIALOGUE 5

YOU: *"What I most appreciate about our relationship is how straight you are with me. As long as you know I care and that I'm there for you if you ever need me, that is all that matters to me.*

I have a lot of respect for you and admire your business savvy. I was wondering if you might provide some insight for me. If you were me, how would you go about meeting more people like you who might have an interest in the kind and quality of work that I do (in your industry, field, profession, etc.)? I would really value your perspective."

Setting Your Goal

The goal of any dialogue you have with your friends, family, and social acquaintances is not to expect all of them to do business with you, but to leave a clear message that you care about them and their finances, and that if they ever need you, you're there for them. In this way, you let them know that your welcome sign is out and if a situation arises, anything from a market downturn to changes in their family or business status, you are available to help them.

The Friends, Family and Social Acquaintances strategy is unique in the Reversing the Deal Flow system in that the "interaction cycle" — the frequency with which you'd use this strategy — occurs whenever you have alone time with key people, and you make it a point to speak with everyone. Other strategies have different frequencies. For example, business development groups tend to have a monthly interaction cycle, whereas client advisory boards tend to have a quarterly interaction cycle.

Set a goal to speak with them until they know you care or they become clients. Continue this technique with new people you meet and you'll soon form a stable base for the additional steps of the Reversing the Deal Flow process.

After reading this chapter, I'd like you to be able to say to us, "Coach there's not a single friend, family member or social acquaintance in my life that I desire as a client who doesn't know that I'm there for them in good or bad markets because I've had a one-on-one direct conversation with each of them and we've directly discussed my working with them to manage their assets." We look forward to that day, to that meeting and the results you will be able to share with us as a result of using this strategy.

Remember to Keep Stats

As with all strategies, keeping statistics is a must. Here is what you want to track when working with family, friends and social acquaintances:

- How many people do you currently know who fit into the category of friends, family and social acquaintances?
- How many out of the total number have you spoken to?
- How many have asked for you to continue the conversation and to see if you might be the right resource for them?
- What are the primary objections you've encountered in this strategy?
- What reframes are having the highest success rate overcoming the most common objections (and what are those success metrics)?
- How many friends, family and social acquaintances have you decided to "walk away" from?
- How many new accounts have you opened within this group?
- How much business have you actually been able to propose to this group?
- How much in assets have you received from this group?

◆◆◆

Reversing the Deal Flow

CHAPTER 8

STEPS 6, 7 and 8

Optimizing Your Book of Business

More, Different, Bigger

A s we move up the marketing ladder, the next set of strategies center on optimizing the revenue from your book of business. These strategies are critical to reversing the deal flow and call upon several rules that Brooke sets forth: "Never call on a stranger when you haven't even called on a friend," and "Don't step over money to make money." In other words, make sure you maximize your relationships with existing clients before jumping ahead to a new marketing strategy.

The steps for optimizing your book include:

- Doing *more* business with your existing clients,
- Providing *different* investment solutions to clients,
- Presenting yourself as an appropriate resource for *bigger* pools of money,

- ***Recovering*** relationships that are lost,
- ***Removing*** non-optimal relationships, and
- ***Repricing*** business.

At this level in the Reversing the Deal Flow coaching program, you will continue to execute on the earlier client acquisition strategies while adding a series of steps that will help you optimize your book of business. The goal is not just to increase revenue, but also to reduce waste and create a more efficient business model, thus enhancing the client experience.

By "waste" we're referring to opportunities available within your existing books of business that you're not optimizing. Waste is created when you maintain a shallow level of engagement with those relationships. Waste also happens when you sporadically and haphazardly market yourself to new people who are not even in your target market, or worse yet, are not in your target market *and* want a massive discount for the pleasure of being your client. You want to be sure your engagement with all of your clients is at an optimum level. This is what makes the entire "eco-system," which includes family, staff, clients, your branch and your firm, survive and thrive. When you give clients your highest level of service, they will reciprocate by becoming advocates of your practice. They will become partners with you and refer people like themselves to you — part of the Reversing the Deal Flow process. ◆

STEP SIX: MORE

Let's start with creating **more** business with your existing clients. Think about the level of penetration you have with your existing clients. Now, take a few minutes to rate yourself, on a scale of 1-10, as to what degree you could be getting more business out of your existing book of clients. A "1" would be that you're managing very few of their assets, and a "10" would mean that you're managing all of their assets. Let's say that you rate yourself a "6." That means you're leaving 40 percent of those assets on the table. (If you use this rating system for all of these steps — more, bigger, different, removal, recovery, and repricing — you will then be able to calculate the average or overall "capacity utilization ratio" of your book of business.) How much of the potential capacity of your overall book of business are you actually monetizing? What percentage are you tapping into based on the overall value provided by these six strategies and starting with **more**.

The next step is to look at the percentage of money you're leaving on the table and ask yourself, "What is my best estimate as to the sum of money it represents?" Think in terms of revenue, not assets. The aim is to come up with a number that is internal to your business. In other words, you calculate the painful number of "how much money are you *not* making from people who already know you and value you because you aren't realizing the full value of that relationship." If you haven't fully optimized all of your client relationships, you are leaving money on the table.

The purpose of reversing the deal flow is not to just expand your client base but to ensure a sustainable ongoing expansion. To achieve that, you can't just do one thing and then move on to the next thing. Instead, you have to create a system for each level. This repeatable, sustainable process will allow you to continually grow your business.

Remember, if you're not optimizing your current client relationships, you probably won't be able to acquire the entire relationship (investments) of a new client. For example, let's say for your overall book of business your capacity utilization *average* is 75 percent. Statistically, that means every time you acquire a new relationship you're acquiring only 75 percent of it. Why? Because you're using the same process with new clients as you use with existing clients.

Ultimately, for each one of these methods for optimizing your book of relationships you will want to follow the same process. You need to have a plan. You need to have a process. You need to know the presentation or script. Then you will be able to handle the relevant objections you encounter. In this book we are focused largely on the presentation and in some cases the objections associated with each strategy. In the coaching we focus a great deal on the plan and the process since "coaching" is all about how you execute, how you perform. The system you use with your current client base should follow the same steps and conversations as those you use when acquiring new relationships.

Here are some dialogues to use with clients when you want them to consolidate their assets with you.

DIALOGUE 1

More: Conversation to Propose Consolidating Assets

YOU: *"Andy, I really do see myself as the principal person responsible for your long-term goals and the investment returns you say you need to achieve your retirement goals.*

"I take that responsibility very seriously and right now I'm concerned. I'm concerned because the reality is, there are factors that I cannot see and cannot control that can have a massive impact on your overall returns. I'm referring to the investments you hold at other institutions. You and I have put a lot of energy into developing an investment strategy, and these other investments, unfortunately, could influence or impact the results of our strategy.

"To be one hundred percent effective, I need to know the full range of what we are dealing with so I can give you a comprehensive set of solutions.

"I would like to have a conversation about moving those investments into our care; that way I can be the person responsible for making sure that everything is coordinated and directed toward the achievement of your goals. I see my role as similar to that of an air traffic controller; I've got to know where all the planes are to make sure there won't be an accident.

"Let me ask you, what do you think about that?"

You could use an alternative analogy to the air traffic controller, such as:

"I consider myself to be a quarterback. To be able to successfully execute the plays, I've got to know where everyone is on the field."

What do you do if you've already spoken with a client about consolidating their assets with you, and the conversation has gone nowhere? You, of course, have three standard options to choose from. They are: 1) change their mind — reframe, 2) negotiate, or 3) walk away. Here is a dialogue for that situation:

DIALOGUE 2

More: Conversation with Clients Who Resist Consolidation

YOU: *"Mike, I wanted to give you a call. Your investments are absolutely fine, and this call isn't regarding your investments. However, I did want to have a very important conversation about our relationship. Do you have a few minutes to chat?"*

Continue to bridge the conversation with a chronology about the relationship you have with the client. Summarize the sequence of events leading up to where the relationship is right now:

YOU: *"So, Mike, when you and I began this relationship going back about [x-number of] years ago, it was necessary for us to put in place the [investment solution XYZ], that ultimately turned out to be exactly what you needed to handle some of the issues that you wanted addressed at that time. I think both you and I felt we had gotten off on a very strong footing. I then shared with you why I thought it could be advantageous for you to consolidate your assets here with us so I could better execute the strategies we agree are going to help you reach your goals. I know that at that time we didn't do that, and I wanted to revisit the subject. Can you share with me what your thoughts are regarding that conversation now?*

Following our standard procedure, your next options are:

1. **Change Mike's mind by reframing the conversation**. Perhaps you did not go about the conversation as methodically as presented in this book. Maybe something has changed about your business (e.g., moving into more of a planning practice, a merger, new staff member or partner). In any case, it offers a fresh opportunity to address the issue of consolidation.

2. **Negotiate.** In this case, it means that you give a little and they give a little. Maybe they won't give you *all*, but they can give you *more*. Maybe there's a chance you can offer a financial incentive or a discount if they modestly increase their business with you.

3. **Consider walking away.** If you know you can't possibly do the right thing by them based on how they want to do business and on the structure and needs of your business, you must respectfully walk away. Your firm no doubt has an automated solution for clients who do not meet set asset levels, or there may be another advisor who is in a better position to serve this client. ◆

STEP SEVEN: DIFFERENT

Different means you are providing as many different types of investment solutions as you possibly can with this client. This strategy not only boosts your revenue, it increases your "stickiness" factor with a client. The more solutions a client has with you, the more likely they are to "stick" with you. Just remember, any time your client is getting a financial solution from someone else, the greater the likelihood that another advisor can take the relationship away from you. Your best client is someone else's great referral.

As with other strategies, you want to rate the number of **different** investment solutions each client has with you or through you on a scale of 1-10. If you rate a client as a "10," that means you've offered that person all the solutions that your firm provides, and those different solutions were purchased through you.

Here is a dialogue addressing the topic of asking for different business from a client.

DIALOGUE 1

Different: Conversation for Expanding Your Solution Offering

YOU: *"Mary, I want to have a conversation with you regarding a specific way I want to begin thinking about our investment relationship. Your current investments are fine, but do you have a couple of minutes for a thoughtful conversation?"*

Mary: *"Yes."*

YOU: *"You know, Mary, it's not unusual for me to begin a relationship by addressing a particular problem, like I did with you.*

"I have a basic philosophy which is, I'm always committed to giving people what they want before I come to them for further conversation about what I think they need.

"I believe we've addressed your concerns in the past. At the same time, at this stage I typically have a conversation with clients and share with them the range of solutions I prefer to be responsible for and which is really the strength and the primary role we play in peoples' lives."

You now move on to "What's in it for them."

YOU: *"Having these additional solutions makes it much more likely we will achieve your ultimate goals, and we'll be able to do it in a comprehensive way. You won't have to manage resources that are scattered elsewhere and, quite frankly, that I'm better equipped to manage. What's your reaction to that?"*

You want clients to know that you and your firm can simplify their lives by letting you handle all of their investment needs under one roof. This is a win-win for both of you. You help your clients achieve their goals, and you bring in addition assets to grow your practice. ◆

STEP EIGHT: BIGGER

Bigger means going after the biggest "size" of business you can ask for from your clients. At what point do you start feeling uncomfortable asking for a certain investment amount: $1 billion, $100 million, $1 million? The limitations you see when asking for bigger business from a client rarely have anything to do with them and everything to do with you. You want to develop a script that makes you feel comfortable and confident asking for a large amount of business from clients.

This means that among your clients there are those who have substantial assets with another firm or advisor. Rate them according to your discomfort or "choke" factor. On a scale of 1 to 10, rate yourself a "10" if you are asking for the most amount of money that would be appropriate for a given investment. What is the largest amount of money you have asked for in a single investment?

In some cases this is a rebranding issue, because the client may think of you as their stopgap advisor or what we used to call a "baby broker." While this may have been the case when you began the relationship, it is probably no longer justified. Sometimes advisors who are in retail will "reopen" bigger cases by bringing in a specialty resource, such as partnering with a private wealth team at their firm to assist clients who have specific needs related to their business, or they will bring in their firm's specialists and/or senior management to convey the firm's capability to handle "bigger" business.

Here are some dialogue openings to help you ask clients about bigger business:

DIALOGUE 1

Bigger: Asking the Client to Step Up

YOU: *"You know, Harry, I want to have a conversation with you about our investment relationship. Your investments with me are fine, but I want to share with you a conversation that I often have with individuals like yourself at this point in our relationship. Do you have a couple of minutes to talk?"*

DIALOGUE 2

Bigger: Repositioning Yourself

Here is another option:

YOU: *"Harry, when you and I first connected, you were referred to me by someone I think quite highly of. I was definitely working to do the right thing by you, and I wanted to do the right thing by them. I was completely willing to begin our relationship on a modest basis which is what we decided to do as a way of getting to know each other better. At this point in the relationship though, I do have to let you know that when individuals have the kind of means that you do, I'm fundamentally their primary if not their only advisor, and I typically manage the bulk of their assets. Of course, right now that's not the case with you.*

"So I'd like to have a conversation with you about that. I'd like to know what I need to do or what do you need from me so I can compete for that business?"

If you think about it, you have nothing to lose and everything to gain. Even if the conversation goes nowhere, the client gets the message that they're important to you. If it goes somewhere, it could result in huge rewards. One of our coaching clients handled a client conversation this way, and he ended up with a $1 billion account that took his production to the eight-figure range. ◆

A Repeatable Process

More, Different and Bigger are the easier conversations in the book-optimizing process when compared with Recovery, Removal and Re-pricing. In our coaching program, we go over multiple scenarios that can be handled with a variety of scripts. We present the appropriate reframes to change a person's mind and help advisors learn the most effective dialogue to use when they have to negotiate or walk away. The main thing to remember is, this is a repeatable process. The scripts are modified specifically for current clients and the new clients you are bringing on board.

◆◆◆

Reversing the Deal Flow

CHAPTER 9

STEPS 9, 10 and 11

The Three R's of Client Management

Recovery, Removal, Repricing

STEP NINE: **RECOVERY**

Hearing from a client who wants to take his or her business elsewhere can be a blow to an advisor's ego and practice, particularly if that client has a large portfolio. It's hard not to take it personally, but if you want to recover a relationship, you can't let your shock turn to resentment or anger. Instead, you want to make sure your **recovery** conversation has the right tone and appeal.

Typically when a client says, "I'm moving my account," what does the advisor say? *"Look, I understand. I know we've had our challenges, but if you look at the overall performance, I think you'd agree that you didn't take my recommendation on some of the things I suggested. If you had, you would have made more money."*

That, of course, is the wrong way to recover a relationship. It sounds accusatory, and the advisor is placing blame on the client. Instead, here are some more appropriate dialogues you can use with a client who plans to leave:

DIALOGUE 1

Recovery Conversation

Sam: *" I just want to let you know that I'm moving my account."*

YOU: *"Wow. That really caught me by surprise, and it saddens me to hear."*

Your reaction should be natural. If that's how you feel, that's what you should say. Most likely you've been blindsided by their decision to leave, and it's disingenuous to help them feel comfortable about it. You don't want to say something like, "I understand." Why would you understand if somebody's going to leave you? Instead, you want to have an appropriate emotional response. Understand that if you in any way blame them, it will only push them farther away. So never say something like "You hurt me" or "I'm disappointed in you."

DIALOGUE 2

YOU: *"I'm really disappointed in me that you had to resort to moving the account because you were in some way, shape, or form clearly unhappy with me. As a courtesy, I'd really appreciate the opportunity to learn from my mistakes; can you share with me what I did wrong?"*

In this conversation, you presume you did something wrong. That's because most people who leave want to pretend as if there's nothing wrong. If nothing is wrong, why are they making a change? You want to presume responsibility, and put them in the position of having to explain why they are unhappy with you. This is the only way to recover this relationship because you cannot retain their business if they will not have an open and honest conversation with you.

The following story helps to illustrate the value of these dialogues. During a webinar we were conducting, advisors we coach were sharing some of their incredible successes when one advisor on the call simply dropped off, rejoining us later in the call. As Brooke and I were wrapping up, he asked if he could speak. He went on to explain that he had dropped off because a client called to say he was moving his account. The advisor said he used the above script verbatim and the client not only agreed to stay, but he apologized for considering leaving.

When a client tells you they want to move their account, take the opportunity to express your true feelings about their decision and take the time to uncover why. Using appropriate dialogue can be a game changer and result in a renewed relationship. ◆

Brooke's Notes

One of our longstanding coaching clients, an advisor and a family friend, adds this postscript to his emails, "Surround Yourself with Great People."

As you add relationships like a coach, daily accountability partner, a coaching team, a Client Advisory Board or mentors, you will indeed be surrounding yourself with "great people." As you remove relationships, activities and thoughts that don't align with your purpose, there is a natural, unconscious growth in character.

The other half of our friend's quote, "Surround yourself with great people," should then read, "and then work like the dickens to provide value and improve their lives."

STEP TEN: REMOVAL

As you grow and refine your practice, you'll often find you've accumulated clients who are no longer a fit or who may be putting an economic or undue service burden on your business and your staff. You may even have clients who are simply a challenge and unenjoyable to work with. If you haven't already done so, it's time to shed those types of clients.

If that advice has a mercenary tone, let's be clear that if you can't give a client the attention they need, you're not doing them a favor by pretending to be the right advisor for them. The advisors we coach are some of the most self-sacrificing people you'll meet anywhere. Unfortunately, that well-intentioned trait can result in holding onto clients they can't fully serve, yet they feel guilty about letting them go. This clearly benefits no one — not the client, you, your family or your firm.

Letting go of client relationships can be painful. However, those relationships can damage your business by putting a strain on your time and financial resources. While doing this is challenging for many advisors, using the Reversing the Deal Flow process provides the solutions for removing non-optimal relationships, and instead adding relationships that force you to grow and improve. It's a simple principle.

You have to take action. To start with, you need a way to identify which clients are beneficial to your business and which clients are creating a burden.

It's natural to not want to let people down even though they are not a good fit for your practice. Unfortunately, you probably feel compelled to give them your all through good markets and bad ... especially bad.

Why is this a problem? Because you may be unaware that some of your better clients are being underserved at the expense of your less-than-optimal or dysfunctional relationships.

Perhaps you justify keeping clients you should remove because you don't want to hurt their feelings. However, the issue may not be about the pain you are afraid to cause others, but a desire to not feel like "the bad guy." Perhaps the real reason for holding on to an undesirable client relationship may have nothing to do with the client and everything to do with you and your concern about your own self-image.

The challenge with growth is that you have to shed your old skin. Yes, it's painful, but not doing something about it can be more painful. The only way to handle the pain is to handle the issues head on. Out of respect for yourself and your love for the people you serve, it is important for you to be crystal clear about whom you can and can't serve.

Identify Non-optimal Clients

In our coaching, we use a scale to help advisors determine which clients are non-optimal relationships:

Above the line is your account or revenue minimum, which is needed for a relationship to be profitable and so you can give it the time it deserves to ensure the best financial outcome. Other factors above the line are wealth, network of contacts, trust and enjoyment, in that

Exhibit 9.1

The Advocate Scale

▲ Enjoyment
Trust
Network of Contacts
Wealth
Profitability
profitable   (account or revenue minimum)
──────────────
not profitable
Cost Money
Cost Money & Time
Cost Money, Time
▼   & Self Esteem

order. The clients who reach the top of this scale are often the people who are best equipped to be your brand advocates.

Below the line are clients who are costing you money. They are not profitable relationships from a purely economic business point of view. The first level below the line is labeled "cost money," as in, "it costs you money to have this client." This does not mean that you need to get rid of these people. Sometimes these people are friends or family members. Sometimes, as your business grows, you want to give back, and these are the people you're giving back to. Don't assume if clients fall below the line, they must be removed.

Personally, I think some advisors don't realize that one way they are actually fulfilling their charitable desire is to work hard for people who can't really afford their services. Doing so feeds their purpose and reminds them why they're in this business and the positive impact they can have on a person's life. As long as these relationships are rewarding and not a major drain on time, there's no reason to let them go and there's no reason to feel bad for having a reasonable number of them, as far as I'm concerned.

Below "cost" is the word "time." These are people who cost you time *and* money. Remember, you can typically make back money, but you can't recoup time. This is a much more serious issue. You need to have a conversation with these clients about how you're going to service them, and you need to get them on the same page with you regarding their use of your time.

On the next line is the word "self-esteem." These are clients who must be removed because they not only cost you money and time, they take the enjoyment out of your job. The key to a successful process is to be able to engage in actions that bring out the best in you and the people around you. People who drag you down are not a part of this system. The system is about reversing the deal flow, not playing therapist to people with serious emotional and personality issues who see you as a place to dump their unresolved issues. These are not bad people, just troubled and not a part of this system; they do not contribute to reversing the deal flow.

This relates to another model. This model (Exhibit 9.2) applies to the concept of reversing the deal flow.

Exhibit 9.2

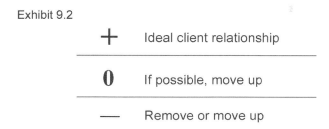

Each of your client relationships can be identified as a minus (negative) sign, a zero sign, or a plus (positive) sign. The diagram above shows that if a relationship is a minus, they either need to be removed or moved up to neutral or positive. The goal is to have all the relationships in your network a positive, with no negatives. If one of your clients is a family member or they're related to a larger relationship, you only might be able to move them to neutral. However, we discourage you from having clients who are negatives.

This system also helps evaluate whether you are doing well. If your clients are doing well, so will you. When clients are a positive, you have to keep investing in them and supporting them in the achievement of their goals. That makes them a more powerful ally in helping you achieve your goals.

Brooke is athletically minded, having trained as a Junior Olympic swimmer and having spent a lot of time around her brother who played for the NFL. Using the analogy of a quarterback, she's particularly fond of referring to a person's greatest asset as their "arm." For an advisor, protecting your "arm" means protecting your emotional environment. Your emotional environment is very much impacted by the company you keep.

As a five-year-old, Brooke experienced what it was like to spend six hours a day training, often starting before the sun came up. She learned that the last thing you can afford to do in a sport where even $1/10^{th}$ of a second can count against you, is to let negative people get into your head, as this would be the kiss of death in the butterfly (her swimming stroke) or any other high-performance activity.

This is not just a statement about clients and selling. The larger model is really about how a person can achieve peak performance in life. You'll find that people who train for the Olympics or take on other major endeavors don't leave room in their lives for people who are negative, and they don't have time for people who are neutral. Everyone they interact with forwards their purpose in life, and that is what makes them world champions. It can be no other way for them.

If you combine both the diagrams, the people who cost you money, time and enjoyment are at the level of the negative sign. Again, if they cost you money and time and you still enjoy the relationship, handle the time issue. Take it from a negative to a neutral. If they cost you money, you could label that as charitable giving, and that could actually move it into the positive. When you implement this client classification process, you avoid accumulating a bunch of relationships that you get mired in managing. You're not eliminating people because you no longer have a need for them. Instead you are removing people because, point blank, as a professional you know you can't provide them the level of service they deserve.

Let's say you want to remove a relationship. What would be the *wrong* way to do it? That script would sound something like this (which is what we've heard many advisors say when we test them during our trainings and keynote presentations):

"I know that you and I have worked together for a long time, but our business has grown and we're now working with accounts with a minimum of $1 million in assets. I certainly appreciate you, but I'm

going to have to ask you if we could move you to a different service that we have for accounts your size."

Are you really looking to make an enemy? Do you really think it's a good idea to play the superiority trip?

Seriously, this is a difficult conversation, and because of that advisors avoid having a script and they definitely don't practice what they are going to say. There's a tendency for it to be handled poorly, which leaves the client feeling diminished or put down. This is not done on purpose, but the damage is still the same. You have to be able to let go of relationships respectfully.

Here's the correct way to handle the **removal** conversation:

DIALOGUE

Removal of Non-Optimal Relationships

YOU: *"Jim, I want to have a conversation with you that is a little bit difficult for me. It saddens me."*

Why do you start off that way? If you start a conversation by asking how they're doing and they respond by telling you how great things are, it feels a bit odd when you tell them you're ending the relationship. It will create an emotional seesaw for them. If they do ask how you're doing, what you want to say is:

YOU: *"I'm doing fine, but right now I want to talk to you about something that's really difficult for me, something that really bothers me."*

This is not a happy call for you. It shouldn't sound like you feel fine about ending or changing the relationship. That can cause an emotional backlash from the client.

Marcus: *"Well, what's wrong?"*

YOU: *"As much as I've enjoyed the relationship with you, and as much as it saddens me to acknowledge this, I hold myself to a standard. When I feel like we're no longer able to serve someone, I want to be the kind of person who's up front and can let clients know that. Because of changes we're making in our business, we won't be the best-equipped resource for you. For that reason, I'd like to coordinate getting you the kind of service that you need and deserve. I'd like to discuss various options with you."*

Notice that in this script you haven't created a legal liability issue by suggesting that you're making this change because you haven't been taking care of the client's accounts. You don't want to insinuate that you can't work with them in the future because you've been doing a poor job in the past. That isn't true.

You also don't want to give the impression that "we're doing so well and things are so great, we don't need you." Instead, you are telling the client that you're looking out for them and want to make sure they are taken care of in the best way possible. Otherwise the message that you send is, "I'm looking out for me, even though it's inconvenient to you, and I'm going to make a change." This is also important because some clients are attached to you. If you tell them that you're arbitrarily deciding to exit the relationship, some clients will beg you to keep them. That could be particularly troubling because some of them may even get abusive with you: "Why are you getting rid of me?"

You have to get across to them that it's against your conscience and against your ethics to keep them as clients because upcoming changes in your practice will not allow you to properly manage their accounts. This way, you're letting them know there are no other options and there's no reason to further the discussion of staying with you. You then need to set them up with other options that are appropriate for their investment needs and financial profile. This could mean using the firm's internal systems for managing accounts of a particular size or recommending another respected advisor who is in a position to manage the account the way you would like to see it handled.

Even though you are ending the relationship, you want that former client to remain a goodwill ambassador for you. If someone were to ask them what they think about you as an advisor, the answer from the former client should be:

"Their practice evolved so we no longer work together, but I definitely think highly of them if you're thinking of hiring them as your advisor."

Your goal is to end the conversation on a positive note. Let clients know they will continue to receive excellent service, just through another channel or through an advisor who can serve their financial needs more appropriately. Your goal in this process is to leave people better off than how you found them. ◆

STEP ELEVEN: REPRICING

Lately, while most of the chatter in the industry is about fee compression, at some point in your career you, as an advisor, will have to contend with the unpleasant job of telling your clients about a fee increase or a **repricing** of your services. However, just because the situation is commonplace doesn't mean it's not difficult. Why? You are bracing for the strong negative reaction it could cause – because nobody wants to pay more for something. At the same time, you have to be realistic. The challenges and costs of working in the financial services industry continue to rise. What business over time doesn't have to reprice its products because of rising costs, inflation, salaries, etc.? Bread can't stay at five cents a loaf for a century. It just doesn't work that way.

Yes, there are currently forces that are clearly driving fees down, but that isn't a blanket excuse for not making sure you're properly compensated for the valuable services you provide.

The first breakdown in appropriately charging for your services is typically lack of marketing, or more importantly, a lack of marketing focus. Is your marketing attracting the "right" clients? If you spend time marketing to clients who require a lot of time to service and who don't want to pay reasonable fees for your advice and services, they will drive down the overall efficiency of your business and reduce revenue. If you don't market actively and consistently, I can almost promise you that, by default, over time you will drift toward a client base that nickel and dimes you until you feel like you're working for free… and I doubt you have a nonprofit status in mind.

One of the best ways to handle repricing is to market to prospects who recognize your value and are willing to pay you for that value. For your unique brand, there is a unique audience for which you provide premium value. Interestingly, your best clients are almost always willing to pay more for your service, and that holds true for almost any profession. They understand your business, they appreciate your business model, and they're not looking to devalue it. These are your best clients who often pay you a premium for your service. They don't walk in the door asking for a discount, like a new, less appropriate relationship might.

Remember, clients and prospects need to see and understand the value you provide before they will be willing to accept a change in fees. You must establish your value and be able to defend it. If your clients understand the benefits and rewards of working with you, a conversation on repricing doesn't have to be stressful.

Many advisors have told us that in the past when they have decreased their discounted rate using a negative consent letter, in most cases they've found few, if any, clients balk at the repricing. Of course, as coaches it is our responsibility to train you for the more difficult scenarios you could face when repricing.

Here's what a repricing conversation might sound like with a client relationship that is priced so poorly that there may be negative value in continuing to manage the account. Remember, if you're not being properly paid to service a relationship, then others will suffer because of that inefficiency. For example, working with the wrong clients and having the wrong pricing structure will rob you of time you could be spending with your family. Your best clients will also suffer, as they'll have to pay more to make up for another client's low fees.

DIALOGUE 1

YOU: *"Nick, your investments are doing great. I just want to have a conversation with you about your account."*

Nick: *"OK."*

YOU: *"I'd like to talk to you about a modest decrease that we need to make in your discount. As you know, we're committed to a*

high level of client service beyond just investments, and I wanted
to get your feedback on the reduction we need to make."

The good news is, you want to keep Nick as a client and he is glad to still receive a discount but at a lower rate. The bad news is, some people are unrealistic or want something for nothing. I have never seen an advisor reverse the deal flow because they're "the cheapest deal in town." In fact, advisors who reverse the deal flow are often high-priced, and their services command and warrant that kind of pricing. If your marketing efforts aren't enough to grow your business with ideal clients, you are ultimately playing a losing game.

In Nick's particular case, you are only "slightly" reducing the discount he receives. You have reframed the conversation so that you are not actually "increasing" your fees for Nick. This conversation shows how you can create a positive perspective in a person's mind.

Notice that in the dialogue, you cue up the subject and get a reaction. I would not suggest going into a long defense of why the discount is being decreased because that kind of justification suggests that you feel you're doing something wrong. The goal is to get them talking. For those who have no significant issue, don't create one by over-explaining and putting issues in their mind that otherwise wouldn't come up.

A successful repricing conversation comes after employing a rating system for your clients. (This is the same type of system you've used for other strategies in this book.) We ask you to rate your clients on a scale of 1-10 on how easy it is to have a repricing conversation with them. Give a "1" to the easiest to converse with a "10" to the most difficult ones. Start your repricing conversation with the "easiest" clients. This allows you to build confidence and momentum and to sort out concerns and issues you might anticipate from the more difficult clients (or those you would most hate to lose). Once you become adept at these conversations, you can keep the worst-case scenario of a client departure from even happening because you've prepared for it. And if there is pushback, you'll know how to turn it around so it's not a big deal.

There may be instances in which a client doesn't want to accept your fee change, and repricing becomes a negotiation. If the client is valuable to you, then negotiating is fine.

Here is how the conversation may take place if a client doesn't want to accept a fee change, and you want to keep the relationship.

DIALOGUE 2

Client: *"You know what? If you're going to increase my fees, then I need to actually take a look at doing business somewhere else."*

YOU: (Replay) *"So what you're saying is that at this point you're thinking about taking your business somewhere else because of this change?"*

Client: *"Yes."*

YOU: (Acknowledge) *"I want to thank you for being up front with me. What I enjoy most about our relationship is the open communication. I'd like to make a suggestion to you."*

Client: *"Sure. What?"*

YOU: *"I'd like to recommend that I take our situation back to management. I believe I can make a strong case that this reduction in fees should not be applied to your account and certainly not to the same degree. I'd be more than glad to have that conversation on our behalf, and I believe that it would be a fruitful conversation. Would you allow me to do that?"*

Client: *"That would be great, I want to thank you for doing that, and I really appreciate the way you work for me."*

Using this dialogue, you'll be able to take an isolated case and make a minor adjustment that is satisfying to both parties. Now, if this client is a financially unprofitable relationship, then the situation would be handled differently, and you likely wouldn't want to make such an offer. Instead, it would be a Walk Wway. That will be up to you to decide.

We emphasize that the issue of having to confront a client who doesn't want to accept a price increase actually harkens back to a lack of or inadequate marketing or prospecting. If you have more of the right opportunities, there's no reason for you to tolerate the wrong opportunities.

Conclusion

The six strategies that relate to optimizing your book of business (More, Different, Bigger, Recovery, Removal, Repricing) are steps to ensure your business and organic growth remain strong and profitable. A healthy client base gives you the means to expand your business by layering on additional marketing strategies that give you access to larger pools of the right kind of clients.

If you follow these steps, you will continually expand the number of ways to reach the right people, and hence, the right prospects to choose as clients. If you had the choice, would you really work with someone who doubted your every move and nickeled and dimed you? The goal behind Reversing the Deal Flow is to surround yourself with clients who value you and your services, and they understand when a repricing change has to be made. Remember to surround yourself with great people!

◆◆◆

Congrats!
You're Now a
RAINMAKER

Epilogue

Volumes II and III
Mastering Strategies to Raise
Your Status to Renowned Expert

How does it feel to be a **Rainmaker**? Completing the 11 steps in this book strengthens the foundation of your practice, and by this time you should be seeing your communications and marketing skills paying off for you. Your social network and social media contacts should be growing and expanding, and you should be attracting the kinds of clients you most want by segmenting and optimizing your book of business. Referrals should be starting to flow in on a consistent basis.

However, your journey is not over. In Volume II of *Reversing the Deal Flow*, you'll complete seven more strategies before you earn the title of Dealmaker. In Volume III, the strategy ladder will lead you to the ultimate title of Renowned Expert.

Following are the steps and assessment descriptions that will be covered in Volumes II and III. You can get a head start by again completing the grid on page 146 and rating yourself on a scale of 1-10 to determine how well you are using each of the strategies (steps) you have learned to boost referrals and grow your business. Then continue rating yourself on Steps 12-27 to assess where your strengths and weaknesses are.

Complete Steps 12-18 to Become a **Dealmaker**
(Included in Vol. II of *Reversing the Deal Flow.)*

12. **Referrals from Clients** – Do you consistently, proactively ask for and receive referrals from clients? How successful are you at following up with and converting these referrals into clients?

13. **Client Survey Referrals** – How successful are you at asking for referrals from clients who indicated on a survey that they would be willing to refer others to you?

14. **Centers of Influence (COIs)** – How successful are you at asking clients for the names of their centers of influence and meeting with those COIs to establish a referral relationship? (Examples of COIs: Advisors in the areas of trust, estate planning, insurance, legal help, accounting, consulting, fundraising, lending, investment banking, taxes, real estate, business management, and others who are central to the business affairs of your ideal client.) How much in assets are you deriving from this strategy? What percentage of your business is due to COIs?

15. **Intimate Events** – Are you regularly holding a variety of intimate events that attract a small group of ideal prospects? Are your communications ensuring attendance at the events? Are events attended by prospects who are likely to become clients?

16. **Client Advisory Board** – Do you have a group of clients you meet with on a regular basis to get their advice on how you can become a dominant resource in your market niche and work with other ideal clients like them?

17. **Mastermind Group** – Are you meeting regularly with a group of COIs to exchange ideas on business growth?

18. **Business Development Group** – Have you established a group of COIs who know how to skillfully communicate your brand and message to clients? Do you have a formal commitment to refer prospects to each other?

Complete Steps 19-27 to Become a **Connector**
(Included in Vol. III of *Reversing the Deal Flow.)*

19. **Board of Advisors** – Have you set up a formal group of advisors who have strengths in the areas where you need guidance and accountability (e.g., team management, marketing, etc.)? Are you meeting with them quarterly and reviewing your marketing and business plans? Are you accountable to each other regarding your goals?

20. **Mentor** – Have you identified a professional in the industry who would be willing to be your mentor — someone who has achieved the business success you are striving to reach? Are you being counseled by someone who has already hit the revenue numbers you want to achieve through the same process you are using? Do you meet with this person regularly to ask for their advice and feedback?

21. **Strategic Alliances** – Are you leveraging your firm's resources to identify colleagues you can align with to produce synergies that will increase your book of clients and your assets?

22. **Strategic Partners** – Do you have formal arrangements with COIs to be a primary resource to them?

23. **Networking Group** – Have you partnered with a group of COIs involved in your market niche to create your own networking group of either prospects or other COIs?

24. **Clubs** – Do you belong to a club or clubs where you are in contact with the best possible prospects, and have you been effective at turning those prospects into clients?

25. **Associations** – Do you attend the association meetings of

COIs you would most like to connect with and/or prospects you would like as clients?

26. **Charities** – Do you engage in the nonprofit efforts of your market niche, and are you able to convert prospects into clients?

27. **Connectors** – Have you identified and leveraged relationships with individuals who are central figures in the lives of key prospects in your chosen market niche?

After completing these steps, you are a Connector!

Complete Steps 28-34 to Become a **Renowned Expert**
(Included in Vol. III of *Reversing the Deal Flow.)*

28. **Journalism** – Do you interview professionals and conduct surveys or opinion polls as a way to connect with hard-to-reach prospects, COIs and opinion leaders in your market niche?

29. **Publishing** – Have you published any of your written works (with the approval of your firm's compliance department)? Have you leveraged authors of works important to your prospects and/or COIs to penetrate your chosen niche? Are you supporting COIs who have a desire to publish and who can create credibility for you within their niche?

30. **Public Relations** – Do you have any public relations contacts in your "Rolodex" who provide connectivity to your marketing niche as well as information on how to best reach key prospects?

31. **Speaking/Seminars** – Are you engaged in public speaking? This can mean hosting your own seminars or speaking at the events of others (e.g., associations, clubs, charitable organizations, etc.). Is a speakers' bureau or other resource promoting you as a professional public speaker?

32. **Podcasts** – Are you creating your own podcasts or using your firm's podcasts to market yourself and your practice?

33. **Radio** – Do you have your own radio show, or are you participating as a guest on the radio shows of others to give your practice more visibility and credibility? Are you working within your firm's guidelines to leverage this medium effectively?

34. **Television** – Have you made connections with people in the broadcast media who can provide opportunities for you to raise the visibility and credibility of your practice? Are you working within your firm's guidelines regarding this media outlet?

After completing all 34 steps, you are a Renowned Expert!

When you earn the title of Renowned Expert, you will be at the top of your game. That doesn't mean you can sit back and rest on your past accomplishments. Remember, you must keep fine-tuning these strategies and continually re-check your plans and processes to make sure the referrals keep flowing.

Stay tuned for Volumes II and III!

◆◆◆

Exhibit D

MARKETING/ COMMUNICATION SKILL	1	2	3	4	5	6	7	8	9	10
	Least <				Use of Strategy					> Most
1. Cold calling										
2. Conversing with strangers										
3. LinkedIn outreach										
4. Social networking (face-to-face)										
5. Friends, family and social acquaintances										
6. Getting more business										
7. Different business solutions										
8. Bigger business										
9. Recovering lost clients										
10. Removing non-optimal clients										
11. Repricing conversations										
12. Referrals from clients										
13. Client survey referrals										
14. Centers of Influence (COIs)										
15. Intimate events										
16. Client advisory board										
17. Mastermind group										
18. Business development group										
19. Board of advisors										
20. Mentor										
21. Strategic alliances										
22. Strategic partners										
23. Networking group										
24. Clubs										
25. Associations										
26. Charities										
27. Connectors										
28. Journalism										
29. Publishing										
30. Public Relations (PR)										
31. Speaking/Seminars										
32. Podcasts										
33. Radio										
34. Television										

A Final Word from Sarano and Brooke
Moving Forward

Now that you've finished Volume I of the trilogy on Reversing the Deal Flow, we hope you truly understand that the art of communication, and specifically the art of persuasion, is a profound talent. Those who rank highest in their given profession are inevitably those who are the most skilled communicators. However, you also now know that when it comes to sales, communication skills can't make up for scattered marketing or no marketing at all. Above all, you must be marketing to the right people.

As Brooke says, "You must have someone to talk to, and it helps a lot if they are interested in your services."

In your hands is the first part of your "playbook," which has provided you with the essentials on how and where to find prospects and the best ways to communicate with them. You've learned a process and order, and the field of play has been established.

The next two volumes will raise your marketing levels to incredible heights, but as you move ahead, we don't want you to lose sight of the strategies you have just mastered. These skills are the foundation you will continue to build on. When top producers share their "secrets of success" at conferences, they are often just giving you the tip of the iceberg. In many cases, they have forgotten the bread-and-butter actions that boosted them to stratospheric success in the first place. Don't make the mistake of bypassing core strategies and thinking you can leapfrog to higher levels. It doesn't work that way.

Brooke and I find that a good exercise to help our coaching clients stay on a rational path is to have them ask themselves the simple clarifying question, "What's the point?" In other words, what's the point of worrying about referrals when you're not even optimizing your current client base? What's the point of sending leads to centers of influence who don't return the favor when you haven't even asked your existing clients for referrals. Remember it is not enough to do the right things, you must do them in the right order. As Brooke so often says, "Pearls are valuable, but pearls on a necklace are worth much more."

The key to the success of our Reversing the Deal Flow process is to realize that you're always campaigning. It's critical to build up your base of brand advocates and get your supporters out there spreading your value proposition.

As you reach for the next volume of strategies, it's important to remember that the best brands and the biggest producers actively and aggressively promote themselves. If you're going to compete, you have to step your game up. The best politicians and greatest athletes have coaches. These experts are there to guide them so they can surpass the competition.

Complacency is not an option. You must know how to be patient, resilient, consistent, and systematic. Think of it like running for office. You can't let your guard down or your pipeline of supporters will run dry. The key is to remain proactive.

You can go to any number of conferences and listen to hundreds of experts expound on client acquisition, but nothing will work if you don't take action. Think about how many diet and exercise programs are available out there. Why then does our nation have a serious obesity problem? Losing weight takes commitment, time and energy. When you don't do the work, you don't see the results. Prospecting — just like dieting and exercise — takes a proactive mindset. You can't control the markets, but you can control how much you promote your brand, market your services and sell your special talents to people who badly need them.

Often we come across advisors who have lost their momentum or don't know the next best step to take. They may have spent years doing the wrong things because they displaced the right things. Worse yet, some have been stagnating in coaching programs or with business coaches for years thinking that one day it would propel them to the next level. While they are clearly working with a professional resource and making an effort, their efforts have been fragmented or their coach had no marketing vision.

Here's where Brooke and I can extend to you our expertise in the way of training and coaching. We can help you study, train and practice, and we can coach you. If you get stuck on something, we can help you find the right way to get back on track. Our coaching is similar to training I provided as a media coach for members of the White House and the satellite-broadcast coaching I provided for the former president of Texaco.

We discovered early on in our coaching programs that the secret sauce for achieving success is accountability. Our coaching clients know that they don't progress by hearing someone pontificate on how to reach your goals. The real results come when they're held accountable for their actions and goals.

You can read more about the power of accountability in my book *The Game: Win Your Life in 90 Days* which is available at my website. It took many years to perfect the system outlined in the book. It was the basis for two television shows that can still be seen on YouTube: VH1's *Broke and Famous* and ABC TV's *The Game: Winning at Life.* They show the documented results of the power of *The Game.*

The process became well known in the financial services industry when we were issued a challenge by a blue chip financial services firm to increase the new account openings of 300 of their advisors.

These 300 advisors had opened only eight new million-dollar accounts (called "A" relationships) over a 90-day period. We put that entire group through our 90-day game process and helped them bring in $632 million in new accounts during that time period. That was a 7,000% increase.

We served as coaches and trainers for those advisors and held weekly calls with them. Everyone who works with us is required to track certain statistics and report them on a weekly basis. Everyone is accountable on a daily basis to an accountability partner.

This three-volume book will give you what you need to excel and reach the Renowned Expert advisor status. However, if you ever feel like you need additional coaching or training, whether in a team setting or individually, The Kelley Group is here to assist and support you. Our purpose is to help the best advisors build the biggest brands and to help them make a huge, positive difference for their staff, families, firms and society.

We'll help you become the dominate player in your market niche or geographic area. We help you become the go-to resource for the prospects you most want to work with. Establish your dominance and demonstrate your supremacy. Go ahead, reverse the deal flow and never look back.

◆◆◆

Kelley Group Services

Keynote Speaking

The Kelley Group is a leading provider of speaking, coaching and training services to the financial services industry. With 30 years in the business, Sarano Kelley has been repeatedly ranked the No. 1 speaker at many industry conferences, including the Securities Industry Association Wharton School of Business program for the leadership of financial services companies.

Brooke Kelley, a speaker and coach for more than a decade to the industry's most successful advisers is emerging as one of the top female thought leaders in the industry. Her insights are particularly important at a time when many firms are striving to increase the diversity of their advisor salesforces.

To book Sarano and or Brooke for your conference,
go to www.thekelleygroup.net.

Coaching Programs

The Kelly Group offers an 18-month Reversing the Deal Flow training program modeled after the strategies covered in this three-volume book. The program, which has systematically created some of the greatest marketing successes in the industry, contains advanced information and practices not contained in the book. Through the program, you will systematically build your social network and add from 10 to 100 times the number of current "brand ambassadors" actively promoting your practice.

To join or learn more about the Reversing the Deal Flow training program, go to www.thekelleygroup.net.

Training

Sarano and Brooke Kelley are leading trainers in presentation and sales skills for the financial services industry. They offer a two-day hands-on, workshop on a quarterly basis. This video-based training program also is available to advisors who work in a branch setting. In addition, the program can be conducted in breakout sessions at conferences. The information covered during the workshop will be the subject of an upcoming book titled *Selling: The Contact Sport and Numbers Game*.

Sarano and Brooke have conducted presentation-skills training for management teams, specialists and various departments of leading advisory and asset management firms.

Train the Trainer — Sarano and Brooke Kelley are also available for training and coaching internal staff.

For more information on customized programs, go to www.thekelleygroup.net.

Books

- *The Game: Win Your Life in 90 Days*
- *A Guide to the Recruiting Conundrum: A Consistent, Disciplined Approach to Attracting Top Talent*

Future Book Releases

- *Reversing the Deal Flow Volume II: From Rainmaker to Dealmaker*
- *Reversing the Deal Flow Volume III: From Connector to Renowned Expert*
- *Selling: A Contact Sport and Numbers Game*
- *The Game: Win Your Life in 90 Days (2nd Edition-Revised)*